Montessori and Early Childhood

Montessori and Early Childhood

A Guide for Students

Susan Feez

Los Angeles | London | New Delhi
Singapore | Washington DC

First published 2010

SAGE Publications Ltd
1 Oliver's Yard
55 City Road
London EC1Y 1SP

SAGE Publications Inc.
2455 Teller Road
Thousand Oaks, California 91320

SAGE Publications India Pvt Ltd
B 1/I 1 Mohan Cooperative Industrial Area
Mathura Road
New Delhi 110 044

SAGE Publications Asia-Pacific Pte Ltd
33 Pekin Street #02–01
Far East Square
Singapore 048763

Library of Congress Control Number: 2009927167
British Library Cataloguing in Publication data

A catalogue record for this book is available from the British
Library

ISBN 978–1-84787–515-0
ISBN 978–1-84787–516-7 (pbk)

Typeset by Dorwyn, Wells, Somerset
Printed in Great Britain by CPI Antony Rowe, Chippenham,
Wiltshire
Printed on paper from sustainable resources

Contents

Acknowledgements

Sincere thanks are due to Montessori colleagues and friends who have been so generous with their expertise and advice: Sue Birdsall, Fiona Campbell, Kathryn dalla Fontana, Peter Erskine, Catherine Harding, Micaela Kuh, Karen Leo, Jeni Peterson, Lucy Reynolds and Raji Sivapalan. I am especially grateful for their observations of children at work that have become case studies in this book. A big thank you to the children in my own classes who feature so much in these pages as well!

I would like to acknowledge the AMI Montessori trainers who over the years, both directly and indirectly, have had the strongest influence on my interpretation of Montessori education, including Liz Hall, the late Camillo Grazzini, Baiba Krumins Grazzini, Judi Orion, Dr Jean Miller and Dr Annette Haines. Any limitations in the interpretation of the Montessori approach in this book are, of course, my own. A special thank you to Lynne Lawrence for reviewing and commenting on the final manuscript.

Finally, thank you to my colleague Dr Helen Edwards, lecturer in Early Childhood Education at the University of New England, for her invaluable advice and support. Thanks also to Jude Bowen, Senior Commissioning Editor, and Amy Jarrold, Assistant Editor at SAGE, for their help.

About the author

Susan Feez is a Lecturer in the School of Education at the University of New England (Armidale, NSW, Australia), teaching in the area of language and literacy education. She has worked as a classroom teacher of language, literacy and English for speakers of other languages (ESOL) across the primary, secondary and adult education sectors, and as a teacher educator and curriculum consultant.

Susan holds two diplomas in Montessori education from the Association Montessori Internationale (AMI) – Casa dei Bambini (Sydney) and Elementary School (Bergamo, Italy) – and has worked in a range of Montessori classrooms. For her PhD in Semiotics from the University of Sydney, Susan analysed the distinctive objects found in Montessori classrooms to investigate how these objects mediate educational meanings for young children. Her research interests include Montessori education, educational linguistics, curriculum design, literacy pedagogy and social semiotics.

Key for icons

Chapter objectives

Activity

Case study

Reflection point

Questions for discussion

Summary

Things to think about

Introduction

The freely chosen spontaneous activity of young children, the activity adults call play, is arguably the foundation stone on which the contemporary field of early childhood education is built. At the dawn of the twenty-first century it seems unremarkable that play is seen as so critical to the development of young children. There is some variation in the ways early childhood educators interpret the activity of young children, and in the ways they respond to it, interact with it, and even name it, but a common thread is the high value placed on play, the spontaneous activity of young children.

A century ago the spontaneous activity of young children, particularly those of less privileged backgrounds, was perceived by some as either animal instinct or the manifestation of original sin. Perceptions such as these led to the belief that a child's activity needed to be 'civilized', and that a child's will needed to be 'broken', if the child were to grow up fit for human society (de Winter, 2003: 168). That this view has been overturned in the last hundred years is, in part, a consequence of the pioneering work of a remarkable educator, Dr Maria Montessori.

So much of what we take for granted in early childhood centres and classrooms around the world only became commonplace with the spread of Dr Montessori's ideas in the first decades of the twentieth century. When, in her first schools, Dr Montessori placed young children from the slums in clean, spacious, well-ventilated rooms, with windows low enough for the children to look outside, with accessible outdoor areas and with furniture and equipment adjusted to the size of the children, this approach was considered innovative, even revolutionary. Not only that, Dr Montessori monitored the physical well-being of the children in her care, regularly measuring height and weight, and concerning herself with the children's nutrition and exercise.

Most amazing of all to her contemporaries, Dr Montessori implemented methods through which young children learned social skills and academic knowledge to levels way beyond what was considered possible, even appropriate, for children so young and with such poor prospects. What left her contemporaries incredulous was that Dr Montessori achieved these outcomes by giving children the freedom to choose their own activity. People of that era could not believe that very young children from impoverished backgrounds loved going to school and were able to learn so quickly through their own freely chosen activity.

This book explores early childhood education through the lens of the educational approach designed by Dr Maria Montessori a century ago. This exploration is based on two proposals.

First, the book proposes that Maria Montessori's ideas have had a much greater influence on early childhood education than is often recognized. By exploring the ways Maria Montessori's ideas have influenced early childhood education as it is practised today, the book draws attention to the history of the profession. Understanding more about the history of early childhood education provides today's practitioners with the opportunity to build a deeper and more reflective understanding of their field.

Second, the book puts forward the argument that Dr Montessori's insights maintain their relevance today. The evidence for this argument is that, one hundred years since its inception, the Montessori approach continues to be implemented in Montessori schools around the globe, throughout Europe, Asia, Africa, the Americas, Australia and New Zealand. Using Dr Montessori's insights to review the field of early childhood education throws practitioners everywhere a challenge, and with it, an opportunity to enhance and extend their professional repertoire and expertise. For those working in Montessori schools this may mean re-evaluating more rigorously and reflectively the principles that guide their practice. For others, who are training or working in the field of early childhood education, it may mean re-evaluating and expanding the possibilities of their practice by learning more about its history and its potential.

Chapter 1 introduces Dr Maria Montessori, a woman ahead of her time, and tells something of the story of her fascinating life. During her lifetime Dr Montessori achieved more independence than was usual for women of her time. Her belief that the urge to be independent drives children's development is the foundation of her pioneering approach to education.

Chapter 2 begins with a visit to a Montessori classroom for children aged from three to six years. This visit is recalled in case studies throughout the book to illustrate key concepts as they are introduced. The chapter then reviews children's spontaneous activity as it is interpreted through the eyes of a Montessori-trained adult. Montessori teachers are trained to observe children's freely chosen activity very carefully. They use these observations as a guide when they prepare the learning environment.

Chapter 3 explores how Montessori classrooms are prepared to give children as much freedom as possible. These carefully prepared learning environments are equipped with beautifully designed materials. The environment and the materials play a key role in generating the spontaneous, independent and purposeful activity that is such a feature of effective Montessori classrooms. This type of activity, according to the Montessori tradition, helps children develop the ability to concentrate, so important to later achievement at school and beyond.

Chapter 4 introduces the exercises that lay the foundation for the freedom children are given in Montessori classrooms. These exercises are called the exercises of practical life. Through these exercises not only do children gain independence, they also develop the ability to regulate themselves, an ability called willpower in the Montessori tradition.

Chapter 5 introduces some of the most iconic Montessori materials, the materials Dr Montessori designed for children to train the senses. The exercises of the senses lay the foundation for the development of the intellect and of educational knowledge. They do this by helping children to organize, categorize and catalogue in abstract categories, the myriad impressions of the world they have gathered through their senses.

Chapters 6, 7 and 8 review how the Montessori curriculum introduces young children to language, mathematics and the natural and social sciences. These chapters demonstrate how children's freedom and independence in the learning environment, combined with developing abilities in concentration, self-regulation and abstraction, are used as the foundation for the development of educational knowledge.

Chapter 9 locates the Montessori approach in a broader historical context. It links her contribution to the field of early childhood education with contributions by her predecessors and contemporaries, including Froebel and Dewey, Piaget and Vygotsky. This chapter concludes with ways Montessori ideas might contribute to the field of early childhood education in the future.

How to use this book

This book has been written for practitioners in the field of early childhood education and for those training to be early childhood educators. Specifically, it provides an overview of the Montessori approach to children's development with reference to the following age groups:

- from birth to three years
- from three to six years
- from six to nine years.

Each section of the book includes relevant quotations from Maria Montessori's lectures and books, explanations of key Montessori concepts and activities you can try out for yourself.

Quotations

Throughout the book there are quotations taken from the writing of Maria Montessori. Maria Montessori was lecturing and writing in the first half of the twentieth century, mostly in Italian. Her writing and lectures were translated into many languages. Most editions of Montessori's writing published in English today are based on the original, early translations. For this reason, the language can sound very old-fashioned. These old translations, nevertheless, retain some of the compelling and poetic oratory Maria Montessori was famous for in her day. In these quotations we can hear echoes of the immense reverence and awe Dr Montessori communicated to her audience whenever she spoke about young children hard at work building the adults of the future.

One feature of the old-fashioned language used in the translations of Dr Montessori's words is the use of the pronouns 'he' or 'it' to refer to the child, where today we would use gender-inclusive language. The original usage has been retained in the quotations used throughout the book for reasons of historical accuracy. It is worth remembering, however, that Dr Montessori's life and work remains an inspiration for woman and girls everywhere, in fact for anyone who dreams of breaking through arbitrary social barriers in order to make a lasting contribution.

Key concepts

When Montessori educators talk about their work with each other, they use many concepts that are unfamiliar to other early childhood educators. Some of these concepts are introduced in this book.

Maria Montessori was one of the first people in the modern era to observe young children closely. She often observed and tried to explain phenomena other people had never recorded before or had never taken seriously. To describe these phenomena, she used the terms and idioms of her era. Whenever you are introduced in this book to a distinctively Montessori description of some aspect of early childhood education, compare this description with the way the same phenomenon is described by early childhood educators today.

Case studies, as well as recollections of the visit to the Montessori school described in Chapter 2, are included throughout to illustrate key concepts as they are introduced.

Case studies and activities

Each chapter includes case studies and activities you can try for yourself. The case studies are drawn from observations in contemporary Montessori schools.

Some activities include questions for discussion and reflection. Readers can use the questions to reflect on the issues explored in the chapter in terms of their own experience, knowledge and practice.

Some activities are guided observations in which you are shown how to observe young children, and the environment in which they find themselves, on the basis of Montessori ideas. You might like to record your observations in a journal. Have your journal beside you whenever you are in a setting in which young children are working or playing. As well as written records, you might like to include visual records, such as sketches, diagrams and photographs (if you have permission).

Other activities ask for your response to the material in the chapter. Your response might include ways for adapting and incorporating Montessori techniques into your own repertoire of practice. Again you could record your ideas in your journal. You will then have an illustrated record of your response to the ideas in this book, ideas you can later use in your work as an early childhood educator.

Further reading and useful websites

At the end of the book are lists of recommended reading and websites you can use to follow up some of the ideas presented in the book. Much of the detail of Montessori theory and practice, however, is not found in any published source. It is handed on to new teachers through lectures and demonstrations during their training. Teachers incorporate this knowledge into handbooks, or albums, they prepare for themselves.

Training to be a Montessori educator

As you read this book and complete the exercises, you will become familiar with some of the principles and techniques used by Montessori educators all over the world. Reading this book and completing the activities, however, will not qualify you as a Montessori teacher.

There is a different Montessori qualification for each of the following age groups:

- children aged from birth to three years
- children aged from three to six years
- children aged from 6 to 12 years.

To qualify as a Montessori teacher for each age group requires at least one full year, or equivalent, of academic study over and above the local qualifications required to teach that age group. To become a trainer of Montessori teachers for each of these age groups requires considerable classroom experience, followed by further intensive international training over several years.

Montessori teacher training courses are offered all over the world. Many of these courses are delivered under the guidance of the Association Montessori Internationale (AMI) founded in 1929 by Dr Montessori to disseminate her ideas and to continue her work. Information about training as a Montessori educator can be found on the AMI website: http://www.montessori-ami.org/. The ideas in this book are based on AMI training courses. The AMI website also has many photographs of Maria Montessori throughout her life, and of Montessori classrooms past and present. You might like to look at these photographs as you work through the book.

1

The Montessori story

Chapter objectives

- To retell the story of Dr Maria Montessori's life.
- To give a first impression of the educational programmes Maria Montessori designed for young children.
- To propose that at the heart of the Montessori approach to early childhood education is the high value placed on children's independence and independent learning.

To be independent is to be able to do things for yourself, to be able to make your own choices and to be able to manage the consequences of those choices on your own. It literally means to 'not hang from' another person or thing. Over her long lifetime Dr Maria Montessori observed young children striving to become independent. She believed the drive urging young children towards independence is the same drive that powers their development. For this reason, Montessori classrooms are prepared so children are able to choose their activities independently. Through these activities, children not only learn educational knowledge, but also how to care for their own needs and for their environment all by themselves. They also learn how to build relationships with others. A Montessori classroom, often called the 'environment' by Montessori educators, is especially designed so a community of children can act, and interact, as independently as possible.

A long and eventful life

The story of Maria Montessori's life is told to English-speaking audiences in two biographies. The first, written by E. M. Standing, was published in 1957, five years after Dr Montessori died. It is a glowing tribute to Dr Montessori and her work by a close friend and collaborator, and provides detail, often unavailable in other published sources, about the genesis of the techniques and traditions of the Montessori approach.

In recent decades the most cited biography is the one written by Rita Kramer, which first appeared in 1976. This biography presents a more critical stance. It provides a broader historical context for the genesis of Montessori's ideas and a more exhaustive, though not uncontested, account of her nomadic and often dislocated life. The following outline of Dr Montessori's life is derived from both biographies.

An independent young girl

In 1870 Italy became a nation in its own right. Many Italians held great hopes for their future as part of a united and independent country. This was the year Maria Montessori was born in Chiaravelle in the Marches region of central Italy, the only child of a well-educated family. She was, according to both her biographers (Kramer, 1976/1978; Standing, 1957/1962), a strong-minded, vivacious and determined child, displaying the kind of independence so highly valued in Montessori schools to this day.

When Maria was about five years old, the family moved to Rome, where she went to school. Maria did well at school because she loved reading and learning. Her love of learning and her independent worldview, perceived as unusual for young girls at the time, is often credited to encouragement from her very well-read mother, Renilde Montessori. However, Maria Montessori did not enjoy school. In Italy, at that time, school learning comprised mostly drilling and memorization. As a child Maria Montessori is said to have declared that she would never be a teacher, nor would she ever become famous, because she did not want children of the future to have yet another biography to memorize.

When Maria was about 10 years old, she contracted a life-threatening illness, but, so the story goes, she told her parents not to worry. She informed them that she could not die because she had too much to do.

Maria excelled at mathematics. In order to pursue her studies in this field, and extraordinarily for a girl at that time, she attended a boys' technical school. She planned first to be an engineer, but eventually decided to become a doctor. She completed her undergraduate science degree in 1892 to a standard that made her eligible to enter the Medical College of Rome, but, as it was unprecedented for a young woman in Italy to study medicine, this seemed impossible. Nevertheless, Maria Montessori persevered against the many obstacles placed in her way, finally achieving her goal, it is said, by appealing to the Pope.

A pioneering medical student

Eventually, Maria Montessori began her medical studies, but there were more challenges to overcome. These included the opposition of her father, who chaperoned her, as propriety required, to and from university, all the while barely speaking to her. When she attended lectures, she could not enter the hall until after the male students had taken their seats. These same male students ridiculed her, and, because a respectable woman could not look at a naked body in the presence of men, she was forced to undertake her anatomy studies alone, working with cadavers in the evening by candlelight.

Despite these, and other, hurdles, according to contemporary reports, Maria Montessori always remained charming and gracious. She graduated as a doctor in 1896, the first woman in Italy to do so, winning academic prizes along the way and establishing contacts with royalty and other people of influence.

A committed young doctor

After graduating, Dr Montessori worked as a clinician in the field of family medicine, especially among socially disadvantaged women and children. Many people in Italy at that time, despite the promise of unification, continued to live in desperate poverty; social dislocation and unrest were everywhere. Housing in poor areas was substandard; malnutrition and diseases such as tuberculosis were rife. Stories are told of young Dr Montessori, not only treating her patients, but also preparing their food, doing housework, and nursing them back to health.

On the basis of her early clinical experience Maria Montessori became an advocate for social reform, particularly as it related to the well-being of women and children. She began to argue that enhancing the quality of the environment in which all children were raised was the key to overcoming the ills of human society, including poverty, inequality, mental illness, criminality and even war. This argument became the foundation of her life's work.

Dr Montessori treated women exhausted by menial work in appalling conditions. In order to feed starving children, these women slaved to earn wages the fraction of a man's, while their children were left without a carer. Dr Montessori argued for the emancipation and education of women and children, for equal pay for equal work, for quality antenatal and post-natal care, for improved standards in housing, childcare, nutrition and education. She was also a passionate opponent of child labour, particularly the use at that time of children as labourers in mines and heavy industry.

The logic behind Maria Montessori's advocacy for women and children seems self-evident to those of us who work in the fields of child health, welfare and education today, but at the close of the nineteenth century these were ground-breaking ideas. Even a hundred years on, at the dawn of the twenty-first century, Dr Montessori's vision has yet to be realized for countless numbers of women and children around the world.

Dr Montessori developed her ideas by using the skills of observation and reasoning she gained during her training as a scientist. Her thinking, nevertheless, was at odds with much of the received wisdom of the day. While influential academics of her era claimed, for example, that criminals and other social 'misfits' were throwbacks to an earlier stage of human evolution, Dr Montessori, in contrast, argued that these people were a product of poor social circumstances at birth and during childhood. Ameliorate these circumstances and the social problems they cause would also be ameliorated.

Young Dr Montessori eloquently presented her ideas at women's congresses and at gatherings of academics, social and political leaders and royalty across Europe. Those who heard her speak say she was a wonderful orator; she continued to give inspiring lectures and talks throughout her life.

An admired academic

Specializing in paediatrics and psychiatry, Dr Montessori developed a keen interest in children who were diagnosed as retarded and disturbed. She believed, contrary to prevailing attitudes, that solutions to the problems faced by these children were to be found through education, rather than through medical intervention. It was through her work with such children that Maria Montessori was drawn to the field of education.

Dr Montessori's work with 'deficient' children, as they were called at the time, led her to attend courses in anthropology and pedagogy at the

University of Rome. Through her anthropological studies, Maria Montessori refined her skills in observation and measurement. She also read widely, becoming familiar with the ideas of the educational reformers who preceded her, including Rousseau, Pestalozzi, Herbart and Froebel. She was especially influenced, however, by the ideas of two little-known French doctors, Jean Itard and Edouard Séguin.

When Dr Montessori was appointed co-director of an institute for 'deficient' children, she implemented programmes which combined scientific observation and measurement with pedagogical innovations from her own and earlier eras. As a result of Dr Montessori's unorthodox methods, her 'deficient' children not only gained increasing levels of personal and social independence, but also began to succeed in state examinations at the same level as 'normal' children. Montessori soon became recognized across Europe as an authority in her field.

During this period, some time between 1898 and 1901, Dr Montessori's son, Mario, was born. Dr Montessori and the child's father, a medical colleague at the institute, never married, so the child's existence was kept secret until he came to live with Dr Montessori as an adolescent. Mario Montessori eventually became his mother's closest collaborator, contributing significantly to the development of the Montessori curriculum, and becoming a leading figure in the Montessori movement.

In 1901 Dr Montessori left the institute and returned to the University of Rome to further her research in psychology and anthropology, both very new disciplines at the time. Eventually, the university appointed her Professor of Pedagogical Anthropology. During these years she travelled, published and lectured, becoming a well-respected academic.

A famous school

In 1907, Dr Montessori was asked by the directors of an urban renewal scheme to open a school for slum children left unattended while their parents worked as day labourers. Dr Montessori saw this as her opportunity to discover whether the method she used so successfully with 'deficient' children could be applied to 'normal' children. The school was called the Casa dei Bambini, or Children's House. It became the prototype for Montessori early childhood education. The experimental work carried out at that school is recorded by Montessori in her most well-known published work, *The Montessori Method*.

The Casa dei Bambini was an environment in which these most unlikely of children from the slums of Rome advanced rapidly in learning, and became sociable, polite and self-reliant. This had been achieved without using rewards and punishments and by giving the children complete liberty. It was as if the children were educating themselves.

If people of that time had not seen the results of Dr Montessori's experiment with their own eyes, they would never have believed they were possible. Dr Montessori's school, and the publication in which she recorded her experiments in pedagogy, became international sensations. People flocked from around the world to visit the school and to learn how to apply Montessori's principles in schools of their own.

Against the advice of many, Dr Montessori abandoned her medical and academic careers and devoted the rest of her life to developing and promoting her educational method. While surprising at one level, this decision is a reflection of just how fundamental Dr Montessori had come to believe educational reform to be for social progress and the building of a functional, healthy and peaceful society.

From the opening of the first Casa dei Bambini in 1907 to the outbreak of World War I, Maria Montessori became world famous, to a degree which was extraordinary at the time. Montessori teacher training programmes were established and Montessori schools appeared throughout the world.

A new educational movement

In the United Kingdom the popularity and success of Montessori classrooms led, in 1915, to the founding of the New Education Fellowship (NEF). The NEF eventually grew into an influential international organization of educators devoted to social reform, individual freedom and world peace.

At the height of her fame, in 1914 and again in 1915, Montessori travelled to the USA where she gave public lectures, published articles, ran training courses and opened demonstration classes. In the United States her work was supported by President Wilson and his daughter, as well as other influential figures, including Thomas Edison, Alexander Graham Bell and Helen Keller. Professor John Dewey introduced her when she spoke at Carnegie Hall.

After World War I, interest in Montessori schools quickly waned in the

United States, but Montessori schools continued to be popular in the United Kingdom and continental Europe into the 1930s, despite many reversals of fortune. Dr Montessori was based for much of that time in Barcelona, but she travelled constantly to give lectures and train teachers throughout Europe. As Europe descended again into war, many of her lectures were on the theme of education and peace. During this time Dr Montessori also travelled to South America. Montessori education continues to thrive to this day in both Central and South America.

In Vienna, Montessori schools were part of a wider social reform movement which so optimistically flourished there from the early 1920s until the 1930s. The first Montessori school in Vienna was established for the children of the poor by a workers' collective of young women. More schools were later opened for children at all levels of Viennese society. Supporters of the Montessori schools in Vienna included members of Sigmund Freud's circle. One of the Viennese Montessori schools was custom-built by a Bauhaus architect.

In the 1920s and 1930s Montessori schools and training centres were established in Spain and France. They continued to flourish in Italy until, in the late 1930s, Dr Montessori refused to allow the children in her schools to be part of the fascist youth movement. By the end of the 1930s Dr Montessori and her family, which now included four grandchildren, had retreated, ahead of the expansion of fascism in Europe, and the burning of her books in Berlin, to the Netherlands, where her method had institutional, as well as popular, support.

The years in India

In 1939, Dr Montessori and her son Mario were invited to India. Influential figures in India, including the poet, Rabindranath Tagore and Mahatma Gandi felt that the Montessori method could be used to help address the needs of the huge illiterate and impoverished rural population in their country.

The Montessoris were in India at the outbreak of World War II. Because they were Italian, they were interned by the British authorities there. By the time they were released, the occupation of the Netherlands by Germany made it impossible for them to return home to Mario's children until the end of the war.

During the war years in India, Montessori continued developing her method, again with the support of influential figures, including Gandhi and Nehru. Montessori schools and training centres operate throughout the Indian sub-continent to this day.

While they were in India, Maria and Mario Montessori developed a curriculum for older children from 6 to 12 years of age. Dr Montessori called this curriculum Cosmic Education because it was designed to nourish the limitless curiosity and imagination of older children and to fulfil their desire to explore and understand the universe beyond their immediate home and family. Much of this curriculum is aligned to the interest the children in the Indian schools displayed for the animals and plants of the natural world, as well as for the Earth as a whole and its place in the universe.

While in India Dr Montessori also began applying her method to the well-being of newborn babies and toddlers. Her ideas for this age group were elaborated after her death into a programme called Assistants to Infancy.

The later years

After the war Montessori schools began to reopen across Europe and Dr Montessori continued her work, developing her pedagogy, visiting Montessori schools, lecturing and acting as an advocate for children the world over, including at the first post-war meetings of the United Nations Educational, Scientific and Cultural Organization (UNESCO), which was established to rebuild a culture of peace through education following the war.

In 1948 Dr Montessori was nominated for a Nobel Peace Prize. She continued working and travelling until her death, aged 81, in 1952. After her death Dr Montessori's son, colleagues and supporters continued her work. The late 1950s saw renewed interest in Montessori education in North America, generating another wave of interest worldwide.

The popularity of Montessori schools continues to grow steadily around the world, a century after Dr Montessori first opened her pioneering school in Rome in 1907. Today many Montessori schools serve children of comparatively affluent families. Through Educateurs sans Frontières (Educators without Borders) the Association Montessori Internationale (AMI) applies Montessori ideas to 'champion the cause' of all children in the world no matter where they live or what their circumstances might be.

Activity

Your own childhood

From a Montessori perspective the child's work in the transition from birth to adulthood is to build independence in the physiological, physical, social, intellectual, economic and ethical domains of life. In the Montessori tradition, independence in each of these domains is seen as the foundation of true freedom. You can reflect on the ontogenesis of independence by reviewing your own transition from infancy to adulthood.

1. At what stage of your life did you become physiologically independent from another? In other words, at what point did the respiratory, digestive, circulatory and other physiological systems of your body begin to function independently? When did your senses – of touch, taste, smell, hearing and sight – begin taking in and distinguishing impressions independently? Over what stage of your life did you become physically independent of your caregivers? For example, when did you learn to walk, to feed yourself and to dress yourself?
2. Describe the process of learning to communicate with others by yourself. Describe the process of becoming socially independent, of learning to build your own relationships and community contacts.
3. Describe the process of becoming intellectually independent, of learning about the world and learning how to learn and think for yourself. At what stage of your life did economic independence become important to you? How have you achieved economic independence? Have you completed the process yet?
4. At what age did you become conscious there was a difference between right and wrong behaviour? Have you completed the process of being able to make ethical judgements independently?
5. What impact did your cultural and socio-economic context have on the way you developed, and continue to develop, independence in each domain of life? How did experiences in early childhood set you up to develop independence at later stages of your life? Did you face any obstacles on your path towards independence in any domain of life? Describe the consequences.

Help me to do it by myself!

From the time a child learns to walk, Montessori educators claim, the child is saying to any adult who cares to listen, 'Help me to do it by myself!' (Montessori, 1949/1982: 136). All Montessori educators keep this in mind as they prepare learning environments and learning materials.

Montessori learning environments are prepared to allow children to be socially and intellectually independent. Montessori learning materials are designed to capture children's interest and attention and to encourage independent use. When children work with the Montessori materials, they refine their perception and their movements, especially manual dexterity, all by themselves. They are also preparing themselves for learning educational knowledge.

In this book you will be introduced to some of the objects and exercises Maria Montessori designed to help children do and learn things by themselves. You will discover how this independence is based on the remarkable developmental achievements of children aged from birth to the age of three, achievements that are refined and extended between the ages of three and six. You will also learn how the independence children gain during the first six years of life becomes the foundation for the rich and extensive curriculum offered in Montessori schools to children aged from six to nine years, and beyond.

Case study 📁

Learning independence
The morning work cycle in a Montessori Children's House lasts for about three hours. The children's morning snack is laid out on a special table and, during the morning, the children help themselves whenever they wish.

A Montessori teacher observed a small child of two and a half, new to the Children's House, sitting at the snack table. The child had selected a whole banana from the fruit basket and had placed it on a plate. The child sat for about ten minutes looking at the banana on the plate.

Because there were bananas in the fruit basket on that day, the Montessori teacher had arranged the following on the snack table:

– a cutting board and a knife children can use successfully
– a container of toothpicks (so children can eat with increased independence or share with others)
– paper napkins
– a bin for food scraps.

After carefully washing her hands in the child's view, the Montessori teacher sat beside the small child and offered to show him what to do. First, the teacher indicated and named the equipment on the table. Then, without talking, the teacher slowly and deliberately took hold of the banana and began to peel it, one step at a time, pausing to highlight moments in the process critical to success. Next, the teacher slowly and deliberately put the peel in the scrap bin and placed the banana on the board. She carefully took hold of the knife so the child could see her handgrip and began to cut the banana into bite-size pieces. Finally, the teacher showed the child how to arrange the pieces on a napkin on the plate, how to push a toothpick into each piece and how to hold the toothpick to take the piece of banana to his mouth. At key points in this procedure the child took over from the teacher and eventually completed the task successfully on his own. When the child had eaten as much as he wanted, the teacher demonstrated how to clean up and how to leave the snack table 'ready for the next person'.

Reflection point ∿

The Montessori teacher saw the child rendered helpless by the unpeeled banana as an opportunity to teach a 'how-to' lesson, a lesson in independence. In the subsequent discussion with the child's mother the teacher learned that the child had never fed himself because the mother could not tolerate the mess he made with food. The mother was amazed when told that the child had eaten the banana on his own without making a mess. The teacher explained that a mess is inevitable when a small child tries to hold, peel and eat a whole banana without knowing how to do it. She described that day's lesson so the mother could follow it up at home.

Questions for discussion

1. How would you respond to a child unable to peel a banana?
2. Think about non-Montessori early childhood settings with which you are familiar. In what ways might teachers in these settings respond to a child in this situation?
3. How much more time does it take the teacher to give the 'how-to' lesson rather than peeling and cutting up the banana and feeding the child herself? Is this a worthwhile use of the teacher's time? Why?/Why not?
4. In what ways has the child gained in independence as a consequence of this 'how-to' lesson? How often do you think the teacher would need to repeat the lesson, and how much practice would the child need, before the child could complete this activity independently?

Summary

This chapter has provided a brief introduction to Maria Montessori's long and fascinating life. It has suggested that the influence of both the historical context and the events of Dr Montessori's personal and professional life led her to place great significance on the development of independence in young children. This chapter has also provided a first insight into how this emphasis on independence shapes the Montessori approach to early childhood education.

Things to think about

1. The Montessori emphasis on children's independence was considered an innovation in the field of early childhood education at the beginning of the twentieth century. What do you think have been the consequences of this innovation for the practice of early childhood education today?
2. How independent, in each domain of life, are young children encouraged and enabled to be in contemporary societies? Consider these variables:
   – the age and gender of the child
   – the immediate setting
   – the cultural and socio-economic context.
3. Identify in your own teaching repertoire strategies you use to give children opportunities to become more independent in specific domains of life.

2

The child worker and the adult observer

Chapter objectives

- To visit a Montessori Children's House.
- To introduce observation as an essential element of Montessori early childhood practice.
- To reveal how Montessori early childhood programmes reflect the stages of child development described by Maria Montessori.
- To explore, from a Montessori perspective, the activity of young children.

Trained as a scientist, Dr Montessori observed phenomena closely as a means of understanding the world and solving problems. When she turned her attention to the study of young children, close observation continued to be her primary strategy. To observe literally means 'to keep near' so you can watch something and come to know it well.

A visit to a Montessori Children's House

The Children's House is the Montessori programme for children aged from three to six years. A visitor will see much in a Children's House that is shared with other early childhood settings for this age group. There are many distinctive features, however, specific to the Montessori approach.

Let's begin our visit.

The Children's House is light-filled, spacious and airy. It has an outdoor space easily accessible to the children. The furniture in the room is child-sized and includes wooden tables where children work alone, in pairs or in small groups. There is a lot of open floor space that is not carpeted. Low shelves are arranged throughout the room. On the shelves are sets of learning materials, each set neatly arranged in its own place.

The children have not yet arrived. A teacher and an assistant are preparing the classroom. The teacher is checking the materials to ensure they are in perfect order. Anything damaged or lost is replaced. The assistant checks that all consumables have been replenished. The adults make sure everything is clean and bright, and in exactly the right place, before the children arrive. One table is a little bit grubby, though, and there are some hand marks on a window but the teacher has specifically asked the assistant not to clean these.

As the children begin to arrive for morning school, the teacher stands beside the gate. Each child shakes hands with the teacher and receives a personal greeting in return. The children put away bags, hats and jackets.

Some children go straight to the shelves and select a tray on which there is a collection of objects, colour-coded to show they go together. The children take the trays to a table, lay out the objects carefully and begin work.

Some children go to a stand and fetch a rolled-up mat. They carefully roll the mat out on the floor and go to the shelf to select a tray of objects, before arranging them on the mat and starting work. One child has fetched a box of large cut-out letters and is using the letters to compose words on a mat.

Some children take a while to settle. They walk around the room, check on classroom pets or chat quietly to friends before choosing what they want to do.

A boy of about four rushes in, throwing his things towards the storage area. 'I want to wash a table', he shouts at the teacher. 'You know what, Josh', the teacher says quietly, 'this table over here really needs a clean'. The teacher examines the table closely with the child. He collects the equipment, which is colour-coded and placed together on the shelf. Although the jug, bucket, brushes, sponges and cloths are child-sized, they are real, not toys, and so completely functional. The jug and the bucket have wide lines on the inside to show the child when to stop filling them with water. The child lays out his equipment, puts on an apron and soon is energetically scrubbing the tables using big circular movements. When he has finished, cleaned up and put all the equipment back on the shelf, with some help from another child and unobtrusive guidance from the teacher, the child seems calmer.

One child has brought some flowers to school today and so chooses the flower-arranging equipment. Soon there are small vases of flowers decorating the tables. Again all the equipment is cleaned, dried and put away, ready for the next person who wants to use it, before the child moves on to other work.

A hum of working children settles over the classroom. Drifting across from the other side of the room is the sound of a child matching musical bells of the same pitch. On a mat in the middle of the room two children are working together with a wooden map of Asia. Each country is a separate piece. The children fit the pieces into the map as if it were a jigsaw puzzle.

A little while later the teacher gathers a small group of children together to give them a lesson. Josh is invited to join the group, which he does willingly. The lesson shows the children in the group how to put away their things in the storage area when they arrive in the morning. The teacher asks Josh to show the others how he hangs up his coat on a hook. Then Josh helps one of the younger children.

After the lesson, the teacher quietly moves around the room, observing, giving more lessons, sometimes to individual children, sometimes to small groups, intervening with as light a touch as possible if guidance is needed.

After about an hour there is an increase in chatter and clatter. Many children have finished their first work. They push in their chairs and carry material back to the shelf where it belongs, ready for the next person to use. Some children seem unsure about what to do next; others are eating and chatting at the snack table. Several have gone into the garden, one child is painting at an easel, one is working with clay and one is looking at books, sitting in a child-sized comfy chair in the book corner. The teacher quietly pushes chairs into tables, tidies a little and prepares for another lesson, observing carefully but not intervening.

A small child notices the hand marks on the window and fetches the window cleaning materials. The child continues cleaning the window energetically long after the marks have been removed.

Soon most children have chosen new work. This time many have chosen a big work demanding more concentration, and the noise levels drop back to a hum.

Suddenly, there is a loud crash. A small child carrying a chair has collided with an older child carrying mathematics material, a box of coloured beads. The box has fallen on the wooden floor and the beads scatter. Both children are a bit shocked, the smaller child close to tears. The teacher looks up, observes carefully but does not move or say anything.

'Can you help me pick these up?' the older child asks. The small child puts down the chair carefully, and begins to help the older child pick up the beads. Soon both children are completely absorbed in the task, the small child meticulously picking up beads one by one, and placing them in the box. There are a lot of beads so this is a big work and other children come over to help. By the time the beads are back in the box, the situation is resolved and both children are smiling.

Towards the end of the morning, the teacher plays some music quietly. The children begin to put their work away. Two children are counting a chain of beads stretched out on a long mat across the floor. As they count, they place small number cards at intervals along the chain. They are not finished, so they tidy up their work and leave it on the mat, placing their name cards beside it. They will return to this work later.

With the music in the background, one by one, the children begin walking around an elliptical line painted onto the floor. The children 'balance' on the line, carefully placing one foot in front of the other, heel to toe. Some children carry objects, such as flags, to add more challenge to the balancing exercise.

To finish the morning, the teacher and children sit together around a large, beautiful rug. They sing a song and the teacher reads a book about a wombat. An older child has just returned from an overseas trip. She uses the globe to show where she went. She tells everyone about a display she has made using things she has brought back from the trip. She has carefully written labels in her best handwriting to put on all the objects in the display. The teacher tells the children that the display has now become another work they can choose during work time. They can look at the objects, read the labels and ask questions of the child who prepared the display.

Most of the children go out to play. A small group stay in the classroom to set the table for lunch. One child brings a vase of flowers to place in the middle of the table. After lunch and playtime the older children return to the classroom. The teacher uses this time to give longer, more involved lessons and to initiate larger projects, for example, in writing and reading, mathematics or science.

The appearance and routines of Montessori Children's Houses vary in response to, for example, the local culture, the resources available, local regulations, how long the school has been established or whether the programme is integrated into whole day care. All Montessori educators past and present from anywhere in the world, however, would feel at home in the classroom we have just visited, and would recognize immediately the materials and classroom procedures. In particular, they would recognize the uninterrupted three-hour work period in which children choose for themselves what work to do, and for how long, when to have something to eat, when to have a rest and when to go outside.

Questions for discussion

1. What is your first impression of this Montessori morning? What questions does it raise for you?
2. What does a Montessori Children's House have in common with early childhood settings you are familiar with? In what ways is it different?

If pedagogy is a science, what does the scientist study?

At the end of the nineteenth century, when Maria Montessori was studying to be a doctor, scientists placed a very high value on observing and measuring the phenomena they studied. When Dr Montessori first began studying children, she carried on this tradition. Her aim was to lay the foundations for a new science of pedagogy, so she devised very elaborate ways for measuring children, their height and weight, the length of their limbs, the width of their backs, shoulders and chests, the distance around their heads, wrists and ankles. She used these measurements to calculate complex ratios and rates of growth, and to classify children into different types.

Dr Montessori's measurements revealed to her that poor nutrition and hygiene stunted children's growth and disrupted their development. At the same time her observations also revealed that, while good nutrition, hygiene and safety were essential, they were not sufficient for children to thrive. Children also hunger after an environment filled with social interaction and sensory and cultural interest, an environment that encourages spontaneous activity.

In many schools in Italy in Dr Montessori's time the design of desks and benches forced children to keep completely still. Observing immobile children in order to study the life of children, Dr Montessori (1912/1964:

14–15) decided, was no better than scientists observing mounted butterflies in order to study the life of butterflies. So Dr Montessori began observing what it was that children did when they were free to choose their own activity in environments filled with interest, without interference from the rewards and punishments imposed by adults. In other words, children's activity became the phenomenon she studied.

More observer than teacher?

In 1913, during a teacher-training course at Ann Arbor in the United States, Dr Montessori told the trainees that 'the teacher in our method is more of an observer than a teacher'. Learning how to observe remains an important component of Montessori teacher training to this day. The importance Dr Montessori placed on observing children led the publisher of a popular American magazine at the time to describe her as 'the woman who looks at children as a naturalist looks at bees' (Rambusch, 1965: 13–14).

Learning how to observe a classroom

When learning to observe, trainee Montessori teachers sit where they will not disturb, distract or interact with the children in any way. They record everything, including small details others might not recognize as being important. In particular, they record:

- everything that interests each child, no matter how apparently insignificant
- how long a child sustains interest in each activity they choose, whether for seconds, minutes or hours
- how a child moves, especially movement of the hand
- how many times a child repeats the same activity
- how a child interacts with others.

Trainees often begin by observing and recording, for an hour or more, everything one child does. On another day, in the same way, they observe and record two children, then, on a subsequent day, a small group of children. Eventually, with practice, they are ready to observe, in fine detail, the activity of a whole class of children.

Montessori teachers are also trained to observe and record the use children make of individual materials over a morning or over a week. In this way teachers monitor which materials continue to capture and hold children's interest and which materials and lessons might need to be changed.

Questions for discussion

1. In what ways do you think careful observation transforms pedagogy (sometimes called the art of teaching) into a science?
2. What aspects of children's activity do you think it is important for early childhood educators to record? Should equal emphasis be given to physical and social phenomena as well as educational ones?
3. What might you discover if you observe over time the ways children use a specific material in the classroom?
4. Would learning to observe children in the Montessori way be a useful addition to your repertoire of skills as an early childhood educator?

In the fields of child health and early childhood education, many innovators and researchers have based their studies of children on observation (Murray, 2009: 138). Observing in the Montessori way approximates the 'fluid rather than static' observation technique recommended by those advocating a sociocultural approach to observing and assessing in early childhood settings (Fleer and Surman, 2006: 145). Where the sociocultural approach foregrounds children's interaction with peers and teachers, Montessori teachers tend to place equal emphasis on children's purposeful interaction with objects that interest them. Dr Montessori, perhaps more than most, emphasized that not only is the true nature of a child revealed during freely chosen, purposeful activity generated by intense interest, but such activity is the basis of all learning.

The enduring Montessori contribution to early childhood education is a series of learning environments full of interest for young children at different ages and stages of development. Montessori teachers prepare these environments and then observe how children act and interact freely within them. Observation determines the help teachers offer children. This work is supported by:

• the conceptual framework Montessori educators use to prepare learning environments and to guide their observations
• an extensive teaching repertoire Montessori educators draw on so that just the right lesson or activity can be offered at just the right moment to any child at any point in a three-year age range and at any moment in a three-hour work period.

Key elements of the conceptual framework Montessori educators use to organize learning environments and to guide their observation of children's activity in these environments are introduced below. This framework underpins the distinctive Montessori orientation to child development and children's activity. Subsequent chapters introduce key elements of the Montessori teaching repertoire.

Stages of development

Dr Montessori's observations revealed an 'infinity of variations' in the way individual children develop (Rambusch, 1965: 15). Emerging from these variations, however, she recognized common developmental patterns. Eventually, Dr Montessori (1949/1982) described human development, from birth to maturity, as a series of four six-year cycles (Table 2.1).

Table 2.1 Stages of development

Age range	Stage of development
0–6	Infancy (early childhood)
6–12	Childhood
12–18	Adolescence
18–24	Maturity

The early childhood and adolescence stages are turbulent, creative periods, in contrast to the stages of childhood and maturity, which, in comparison, are 'calm phases of uniform growth' (Grazzini, 1996: 213).

The boundaries between the stages are approximate only. Because Montessori educators observe children's spontaneous activity so closely, they are able to identify when individual children are in transition from one developmental stage to the next. In this way individual variation is taken into account.

Dr Montessori was careful not to represent human development as a relentless step-by-step upward progression from birth towards adulthood. Such a view of development inevitably focuses on what children are not yet able to do at each step on the pathway to adulthood, portraying them as imperfect adults with deficits to overcome. The Montessori model encourages educators to focus on what children can do at each stage of development and to appreciate the special intellectual power, social affinity and creative potential of each stage.

Montessori educators view development as a process of adaptation unfolding over time as a consequence of a child's active interaction with the environment. Children construct themselves from what they take from their environment. They are able to do this because they are born with creative potential, manifested in the absorbent mind and the ebb and flow of sensitive periods from one developmental phase to the next. 'This is how', Dr Montessori (1949/1982: 166) argues, 'differential continuity is kept going between the various human communities which have evolved each its own civilisation down the ages'.

Questions for discussion

Review models of child development you have encountered in your studies of early childhood.

1. How many of these models describe child development as a series of incremental steps? What other ways are there of modelling development?
2. How would you describe the model of development that underpins the curriculum mandated by your local educational authority? To what extent does this model take into account individual variation and the diverse contexts in which children grow and develop?
3. What insights and possibilities for new directions, if any, does the Montessori description of the stages of child development offer early childhood educators today?

Multi-age groupings

Each stage of development, in the Montessori view, is made up of two three-year phases. In the first phase the special characteristics of the stage build in intensity, before gradually waning in the second phase. Each Montessori learning environment is prepared for a particular three-year phase. Three-year multi-age groupings are, therefore, a feature of the Montessori approach.

The way environments are prepared for communities of infants from birth to three depends on whether the infants are walking or not. The Montessori environment prepared for children aged from three to six is the Children's House. After the age of six children are grouped into two multi-age classrooms, the first prepared for children from 6 to 9 years and the second for children from 9 to 12. Montessori adolescent programmes are prepared for students from 12 to 15 years. After the age of 15 students are ready to participate in educational pathways that lead to post-school education and training.

Questions for discussion

1. What might be the advantages, and disadvantages, of grouping children and adolescents, throughout their education, in three-year multi-age settings following the Montessori model?
2. How are children grouped in early childhood settings with which you are familiar? How do these groupings benefit children's development? Do these groupings pose any problems?
3. What do you think are the advantages of multi-age groupings in early childhood settings in general? What are the challenges?

Sensitive periods

When Dr Montessori studied children's spontaneous activity, she observed that children went through temporary periods in which they were intensely interested in very specific elements of the environment. As children begin each stage of development, new sensitivities appear and increase in intensity and focus for the first three-year phase; then, over the next three years, they gradually fall away until the sensitivities of the next stage take over (Grazzini, 1996: 212).

In the Montessori tradition these periods of heightened interest, called sensitive periods, signal the opening of windows of developmental opportunity. During these transient periods of heightened interest children tend to focus their attention on particular objects and activities, while ignoring other aspects of the environment. Each special interest is so intense that 'it leads its possessor to perform a certain series of actions ... with an outpouring of energy incredible to us' (Montessori, 1949/1982: 44).

When, in the wake of a sensitive period, heightened interest leads a child to focus on an aspect of the environment, the spontaneous activity that followed was observed by Dr Montessori to involve a great deal of effort. Moreover, the child becomes completely absorbed in the activity. If children are left free to continue this activity for as long as they want, when they are finished, rather than being tired, they seem refreshed, calm and happy. Where other observers might describe children's activity of this type as play, in the Montessori tradition it is called children's work.

When a new sensitivity emerges, if children are to construct the corresponding 'function' in an optimal way, they need to find something in their environment to be the focus of their interest and activity. If the environment does not enable a young child to exploit a developmental opportunity signalled by a sensitive period, the opportunity may be lost and the child may find it much more difficult to achieve that same developmental step at a later time.

Montessori educators aim to prepare environments which match the interests of children during sensitive periods, and which, therefore, stimulate children's activity at times when their potential to construct the corresponding achievement, easily and spontaneously, is at its peak.

Today the phenomenon of developmental sensitive periods in infancy and early childhood is being re-visited by neuroscientists (OECD CERI, 2007). Research appears to confirm that such periods exist, but the implications for early childhood education continue to be debated. Montessori educators would argue that tailoring a learning environment to a developmental stage and observing closely a child's freely chosen activity within that environment continues to be the best means for making judgements about how to meet an individual child's developmental needs, sensitivities and interests.

Infancy: the formative period

Infancy, the period from birth to about six years of age, is, in the Montessori tradition, the developmental period of greatest significance. During this time helpless, newborn infants transform themselves into walking, talking children, adapted to their particular place in the world and time in history. In order to help parents and educators gain a deeper insight into this extraordinary period of transformation, Dr Montessori used two powerful metaphors: the psychic embryo and the absorbent mind.

The psychic embryo

The 'psychic embryo' is the metaphor used by Dr Montessori (1949/1982: 52–72) to describe the post-natal period. Just as an embryo needs a special, secure environment to 'construct' each of the organs that will later function to sustain life after birth, newborns need a loving, secure environment to construct each psycho-social 'organ' they will later need in order to function in the social and intellectual life of the human community into which they are born. The development of a child's eyes and ears before birth, for example, is matched by the development of a child's visual and aural perceptions in the period immediately after birth. How an individual child's psycho-social functions develop depends on the interaction between the child's remarkable ability to learn and remember and the material and social environment provided by the child's carers and community. It is from resources available in the environment that children construct themselves.

The absorbent mind

The unique and powerful way young children learn and remember is captured in Dr Montessori's metaphor, the 'absorbent mind'. Young children, she argues, 'absorb' impressions from the environment, and these impressions form the actual fabric of the mind and intellect under construction. What is more, young children learn and remember without knowing they are doing it 'simply as a result of living, without any need for more effort than is required to eat or breathe!' (Montessori, 1949/1982: 22). The absorbent mind enables children to adapt to the unique time and place into which they are born.

The first phase of infancy: from birth to age three

The sensitive periods of the first three years of life correspond to the stellar achievements of this age, learning to walk and learning to talk. In the Montessori tradition these two achievements are closely intertwined. In fact, a distinctive feature of the Montessori approach is the importance given to the role of movement in the construction of the intellect. This is the focus of the next chapter.

The sensitive periods that emerge during the first three years of life are outlined in Table 2.2.

Table 2.2   Sensitive periods in the first three years of life

Age range	Sensitive period
0–3 (peak at 3)	a strong urge to use all the senses to explore the world
0–3	an intense interest in spoken language
0–3 (peak at 2)	a love of order and routine
2–3	an interest in precise, controlled movement
2½–3½	a fascination with very small things

The sensitive periods of this phase ebb and flow. The love of order and routine, for example, peaks at about the age of two when the need to orient the self in the world is at its most intense. A toddler's tantrum is interpreted by Montessori educators as a response to something perceived to be out of place or a familiar routine disrupted, in other words, an assault on the sensitive period for order. Toddler tantrums illustrate just how intensely young children experience this sensitive period when it is at its peak.

During her lifetime Dr Montessori outlined ideas for supporting the development of infants from birth to three years of age. Today there are Montessori Assistants to Infancy who help parents prepare for a new baby. Montessori environments are also prepared for infants and toddlers in day care, and for toddlers accompanied by a parent. Infant communities, as these environments are called, are secure and nurturing places filled with opportunities for independent activity.

The second phase of infancy: The Children's House

While babies and toddlers effortlessly and unconsciously absorb myriad impressions from their environment, from about the age of three the child is 'always playing with something ... working out, and making conscious something that his unconscious mind has earlier absorbed' (Montessori, 1949/1982: 23). From the age of three children bring their understanding of the world to consciousness through their own activity, especially through activity with their hands. During this period the gradually waning sensitive periods of infancy evolve in the ways outlined in Table 2.3.

Table 2.3 Sensitive periods in the second phase of infancy

Age range	Sensitive period
3–4	successive interest in specific types of sensory exploration, one sense at a time
4–5	an urge to refine sensory perception and discrimination
3½– 6	an interest in the customs of their social group
3½–5	an interest in writing
4–6	an interest in numbers and counting
4½–6	an emerging interest in reading

Children of this age are ready to take their first steps beyond the home and family into the wider society. The Montessori environment prepared for these children, the Children's House, is sometimes described as a society in embryo. The materials in the Children's House are offered as motives for activity through which children refine and extend their control of sensory perception, movement and language, the functions they created from scratch in the first three years of life. Through this activity, children learn to be independent in practical, everyday ways.

The Children's House was the first learning environment Dr Montessori prepared, and it remains central to the Montessori early childhood educational programme. Dr Montessori lived through the terrible events that afflicted European society in the first half of the twentieth century. The solution to society's ills, in her opinion, lay with young children aged from three to six. She argued that quality early childhood education is the best way to reform society and to build a peaceful world (Montessori, 1943/1971; 1946; 1949/1982: 58).

Children's activity: is it play or work?

Children's freely chosen activity is described by Montessori educators as their work. The term 'work' suggests an arduous activity undertaken to produce some kind of final product, so it can seem out of place in our era when play, not work, is recognized as 'the foundation for all learning' in early childhood (Waller and Swann, 2009: 40). If children in our time are free to develop through play, it is in no small part thanks to the work of social reformers such as Maria Montessori, who, at the turn of the twentieth century, campaigned for the abolition of child labour. It is worth exploring, then, what exactly Dr Montessori meant when she described the spontaneous activity of children as their work.

Dr Montessori was very clear about activity she did not think was children's work. For example, she was appalled by the 'sorry spectacle' of the schoolrooms which emerged during the Industrial Revolution and which continued to blight the lives of countless young children well into the twentieth century. In these schoolrooms large groups of children were 'condemned', in her words, to sit in dirty rooms on hard benches, listening to the teacher for long periods of time. In Dr Montessori's view, furthermore, the 'prizes and punishments' teachers used to make children pay attention to 'barren and meaningless knowledge' resulted in 'unnatural' and 'forced' effort (Montessori, 1912/1964: 14–15). This, argued Dr Montessori (ibid.: 21), was a form of 'slavery' from which children needed to be liberated.

The activity Montessori educators call children's work is, therefore, certainly not enforced activity. It is in fact a type of activity many adult observers would call play, but with two distinctive features (Montessori, 1949/1982: 156):

• It involves a great deal of purposeful effort and concentration.
• It is oriented towards future achievements.

The use of the word 'work' to describe this type of activity is a mark of the respect it receives in Montessori schools. As much as possible, Montessori educators avoid anything that might distract or disrupt a working child because the child's effort and concentration are understood to be responses to the heightened interest of a sensitive period and, thus, a sign of development in progress. Montessori educators believe that the term 'work' gives the activity through which children construct the adults of the future the dignity it deserves. This activity, after all, can be thought of as the most fundamental contribution any group makes to society (Montessori, 1918/1965b: 9).

Questions for discussion

1. What do adults typically see when they observe young children's spontaneous activity?
2. What is the adult's role in relation to this activity?
3. What prejudices might distort an adult's observation of children's activity? What impact might such distortion have on the adult's interaction with children in an early childhood setting?

The normal state of childhood

When children are engaged, by choice, in developmental work, this is considered, in the Montessori tradition, to be the 'normal' state of childhood. When children are overly timid, passive, clingy, nervous or withdrawn or when children are overly aggressive, destructive or possessive, Montessori educators interpret these behaviours as adaptations children have made in order to accommodate developmental obstacles in the physical or social environment. The solution, from the Montessori point of view, is to remove the obstacles and to allow children to be free to turn their attention to things that interest them, letting them concentrate on the resulting activity for as long as they like.

When a child's behaviour is unsafe, disruptive or distressing to themselves or others, Montessori educators intervene immediately, distancing the child from the source of the problem and guiding the child towards something they know from observation will capture the child's interest and attention, even if, at first, that interest and attention are only fleeting.

Activity

Observe children at play in a range of settings, for example, at home, shopping, at the park or at an early childhood centre. If the play is the type Montessori educators describe as children's work, use the following questions to reflect on your observations:

- What captured the child's interest?
- What activity did this interest generate?
- How long did the child continue the activity?
- Was the child interrupted or distracted? If yes, how did the child react?
- If the child was free to finish the activity in his or her own time without interruption, what did the child do after finishing?

If the play is a type a Montessori educator would not describe as children's work, use the following questions to reflect on your observations:

- What are the features of this type of play?
- Did you observe behaviour that signalled the child was facing a developmental obstacle? If so, how would you describe the obstacle and the child's adaptation to that obstacle? If it were possible, how might you adjust the child's environment to remove or ameliorate this obstacle?

Creativity and imagination in early childhood

The activity Montessori educators interpret as work involves children using their hands to interact with real things in the environment. The emphasis on real things draws attention to a claim sometimes made about Montessori education, that the Montessori approach restricts children's creativity and imagination. This claim deserves a closer look.

In the century since the first Children's House, the Montessori approach to education has been criticized from time to time for not letting children engage in creative and imaginative play. This is clearly a misconception, given the high value Dr Montessori placed on children being free to choose their own activity, activity adults often interpret as play. One reason for this misconception, however, may be the fact that Montessori classrooms do not have a lot of toys.

There were toys in the first Children's House in the slums of Rome, many of them expensive, elaborate toys provided by wealthy benefactors. Dr Montessori observed, however, that, when left to their own devices, the children tended to ignore the toys and chose instead to work with 'real things'. Over the years, her observations confirmed this trend, and toys ceased to be a feature of Montessori early childhood education (Montessori, 1936/1983: 130).

Many Montessori classrooms today include a limited range of carefully selected toys, for example, plain building blocks. The Montessori materials also share many of the characteristics of toys, although they are different from toys in important ways, as we will see in the following chapters. What are not found in Montessori classrooms, however, are toys based on distorted representations of reality, representations often referred to as fantasy. Excluding fantasy from early childhood opens the Montessori approach to the accusation that it stifles children's creativity and imagination. In fact, Montessori educators argue the opposite is true. They argue that the best way to nurture children's creativity and imagination is to bring them into contact with reality in meaningful and rewarding ways.

As with most Montessori principles, the emphasis placed on reality emerged from observing what interests children most. Just as children in the first Children's Houses found real things more interesting than toys, Dr Montessori observed that, more than listening to fairy tales, children like learning about the marvels of the real world, such as a butterfly emerging from a chrysalis, or the parts of a plant.

In Dr Montessori's time, fantasy and play were often used as a means of control. Children were sent away to play by adults who wanted to be rid of them and fantasy was used to terrify children into obedience or submission (Mario Montessori, 1965: x). Furthermore, because of her background in psychiatry, Dr Montessori interpreted living in a fantasy world disconnected from reality as a symptom of illness, not as a manifestation of creativity or imagination. The fantasy worlds offered to children in Dr Montessori's time, as in ours, are the products of adult imaginations. Such fantasy, in the Montessori view, risks depriving young children of opportunities to create their own responses to the real world, which, for a young child, is the source of novelty and wonder beyond all others.

Although Montessori early childhood educators turn away from toys and fantasy, creativity is central to their work. In the Montessori view, the period of the absorbent mind from birth to about six is a period of creativity second to none because children are literally creating themselves out of everything they absorb from the environment. Once children are six, imaginative story-telling becomes a catalyst for learning in Montessori classrooms.

Questions for discussion

1. What, in your opinion, is the role of creativity and imagination in early childhood? How does this compare with the Montessori attitude to fantasy-based toys and stories in early childhood settings?
2. How do Montessori's ideas about the absorbent mind, imagination and creativity resonate in today's world, in which young children can be bombarded with fantasy-based cartoons, movies and picture books, as well as toys and food products derived from these?
3. Can you think of contemporary contexts in which play and fantasy are used by adults to control young children? How is this achieved? Is the outcome positive or negative in your opinion?

The two phases of childhood: children aged from 6 to 12

The 'real' world for children who work and play in the Children's House is their immediate surroundings: all the things they can hear, see and touch. From about the age of six, in the Montessori view, the special intelligence of early childhood, the absorbent mind, begins to make way for a different kind of learning and remembering, one based on reasoning, abstraction and the imagination. Children increasingly exercise their imagination, ask questions, research and problem-solve in order to explore the wider world, far beyond the immediate here-and-now accessible to the senses. The sensitive periods of this age include:

- a heightened interest in being part of a social group
- a fascination with different fields of knowledge
- an urge to investigate ethics and morality and to construct a social conscience.

Children of this age are able to handle abstract concepts, including mathematical and scientific concepts, so they begin to 'let go' of the concrete material they used in the Children's House, although this process may take a few years.

In the Montessori view, 'there is no limit' to what children between the ages of 6 and 12 can explore, 'if the opportunities are there and the conditions are favourable' (Grazzini, 1996: 216–17). Children of this age in Montessori schools are expected to meet the requirements of the local education authorities, but after that they are free to pursue independent study and exploration. As a result, 12-year-old children completing the Montessori programme have often covered material not usually studied until secondary school in other educational settings.

Summary

This chapter began with a visit to a Montessori Children's House. It then explored the place of observation in Montessori practice. Finally, the chapter introduced key features of the conceptual framework used by Montessori educators when they prepare learning environments and observe children's activity. These features include:

- stages of development
- sensitive periods
- children's activity as developmental work
- the normal state of childhood.

Things to think about

1. What preparation is needed if children are to be free to meet their own needs and follow their own interests in an early childhood setting?
2. How does our view of childhood shift if we think of children as workers constructing the adults of the future?
3. If children are workers constructing the future, what is the social role of early childhood education?

An environment of movement and order

> ## Chapter objectives
> - To explore the role of concentration in children's development.
> - To build understanding of the Montessori prepared environment.
> - To propose that the development of movement and the development of mind are interwoven in early childhood.

Recall the visit to a Montessori Children's House described in the previous chapter. Before the children arrived, the teacher and the assistant, very carefully and systematically, prepared the environment. Nevertheless, despite the focus on cleanliness and order, a grubby table and hand marks on a window were left as they were. The teacher's observations over previous days had revealed that some children were very interested in table washing and window cleaning. A table and window that needed cleaning had the potential, for these particular children, to become, in Dr Montessori's words, 'motives for constructive activity' (Montessori, 1949/1982: 178).

Constructive activity is freely chosen activity, work in Montessori terms, in which children use real objects to achieve a purpose. This type of activity involves concentration. When we concentrate, we draw together all our thoughts and actions so that our attention is centred on one activity to the exclusion of all others. The word 'concentrate' literally means to draw together towards the centre.

The prepared environment

Every detail of a Montessori classroom is planned ahead of time with the following aims:

- to give children as much freedom and independence as possible
- to make it possible for children to learn through their own activity
- to provide motives for purposeful activity that requires concentration.

The Children's House was the first Montessori prepared environment. When Montessori environments were later prepared for infant communities, and for older children in the early years of school, the same design principles were retained, but with variations to accommodate the different needs and learning styles of children at different developmental stages. Because the Children's House is the prototypical Montessori prepared environment, we will explore this environment in some detail before we consider how it has been adapted for younger and older children.

Preparing a Montessori Children's House environment

Small children love to find themselves in miniature worlds, environments in which all the furniture and objects are on the same scale as themselves. The Montessori Children's House is prepared to be just such a world, a world that delights children and offers them many possibilities for activity that interests them. From the very first Children's House Dr Montessori (1949/1982: 14) observed that:

> No sooner was the child placed in this world of his own size than he took possession of it. Social life and the formation of character followed automatically.

As they prepare a Children's House environment, all Montessori educators follow the same 'template', adapting it to the local culture and available resources.

- The environment is prepared for a community of children, aged from three to six years.
- The environment is prepared and looked after by a Montessori-trained adult, often called a director, and an assistant.
- The environment is an attractive space divided into separate learning areas.

- In each area there are open shelves on which appealing and meticulously designed materials are placed at the children's level and within their reach.

A community of children

In the Children's House environment children move around and interact freely. A balance of ages and gender across the three-year age range gives the community a family-like feel, the older children often helping the younger ones.

The harmony of this embryonic community depends on a balance between liberty and discipline, that is, a balance between the freedoms each child is given and the limits placed on these freedoms. The children are free to move around the classroom. They are also free to choose their own work, as well as:

- where they work
- how long they work on any activity
- with whom they work and interact.

The children's freedom is limited by the features of the physical space and by the need to maintain social harmony and the conditions that support learning. For example, children are not free to disturb someone who is working or to misuse the learning materials. They are also responsible for returning materials to the shelves ready for the next person to use and for contributing to the care of the environment.

Prepared adults

In the background, but present in a way which makes the children feel safe and secure, are the adults, usually one trained Montessori educator and one assistant. With too many adults the children tend to become dependent on adult help. Trained Montessori educators are not teachers in the traditional sense. For this reason, they are often called 'directors', a translation of the Italian word for someone who guides or draws others together, in the way a conductor guides an orchestra. The role of the Montessori director is to prepare the learning environment and to connect the children with this environment. Once in contact with the prepared environment, children should be able to find everything they need to educate themselves, without unnecessary adult interference.

A Montessori teacher's appearance and demeanour should always reflect what an honour it is to be in the company of children. Every day in the Children's House, for example, according to one Montessori tradition, the teacher should wear something that the children will find attractive, perhaps sparkling jewellery, a fascinating watch or a scarf in rich colours made out of fabric such as velvet or silk.

In Montessori schools all interactions with the children are respectful. Children are never treated like dolls to be fussed over, nor are they treated as a source of condescending amusement or scorn when they behave in ways an adult might interpret as 'cute' or 'difficult'. Montessori adults never talk about children in their hearing, for example, to a visiting parent or professional. If children are present, they are included in the conversation. Even when children are not present, Montessori teachers endeavour to speak about them respectfully at all times.

An artistically beautiful, ordered space

A Children's House has plenty of light and fresh air. It is aesthetically appealing, with simple and elegant furnishings and clean, bright colours. Every effort is made to keep the environment in perfect order, spotlessly clean, and with everything in its place. The plants in the room are healthy and the flowers are fresh and arranged in attractive vases. The overall effect is charming, harmonious and inviting.

The environment has plenty of open space, both indoors and outdoors, so the children can move about easily and freely within and between all areas. The windows are low enough for children to see outside. All furnishings and objects in the Children's House are child-sized, and placed at a child's level and within a child's reach.

Decoration in the Children's House exemplifies the best of the children's culture, for example, cushions covered in traditional fabrics, a beautiful rug for the whole class to gather around, and, on the walls, images by great artists, photographs of valued cultural artefacts and scenes from nature. There are no kitschy or 'cutesy' images or ornaments, nor forgotten bits and pieces gathering dust. The children should be able to distinguish each item in the environment, even decorative items, so they can focus their attention on that item if they wish.

The design of the furniture is simple and elegant. Ideally, furniture is made out of natural materials such as wood or cane. The tables and chairs are washable, and light enough for children to carry to places of their own choosing. Children are able to use the handles and knobs on doors, drawers and cupboards.

The preparation of the physical space takes into account its role as one of the limits on children's freedom. The space incorporates all the safety measures demanded of an early childhood setting, but it also includes some less typical features. For example, the floor is not carpeted. Uncontrolled movements on an uncarpeted floor make a noise, as do chairs or tables moved carelessly, or objects when dropped. Dropped objects may even break. An uncarpeted floor, thus, becomes a limit to freedom, a control of error, telling children when they need to move with more care.

Separate areas

Just like a real house, the Children's House has separate areas, for example, areas for working, for reading and relaxing, for eating and for personal care. The function of each area is reflected in the furnishings and decoration. Traditionally, the tables and chairs in the work area are made of wood, either painted in light colours or polished, and a small comfy chair is placed in the book corner alongside an attractive rug and some cushions.

The workspace in the Children's House is further divided into separate areas, one for each area of the Montessori curriculum for children aged from three to six years. First, there are the two foundation areas of the Montessori curriculum: the exercises of practical life and the exercises of the senses. These two areas extend into an area for manual and creative arts activities. They are also the starting point for children's work in the mathematics and language areas of the classroom. The language area is further extended to include activities that build cultural knowledge and understanding.

Enticing, functional objects

All the learning materials in all areas of the classroom are displayed on open shelves where children can see and reach them. The learning materials are made up of sets of objects. These objects are real and fully functional, most meeting exacting specifications. They vary in colour, shape, size, texture and possibilities for manipulation. Their design entices children to handle them and encourages precise and extended use.

The materials are stored in containers children can carry by themselves, for example, trays, baskets or boxes. The objects in each set, and their container, are colour coded to show they belong together. There is only one of each set of materials and each has its own special place on a shelf. It is not possible for children to choose a set of materials already in use, so they must wait until it has been returned to its place. As children wait for their turn, they learn patience, and, when their turn comes, they are more likely to treat the material with increased respect. Whenever children are shown how to use materials, included in the lesson are demonstrations of how to take the material off the shelf, how to carry the material to a workspace and how, when the child has finished the work, to return the material to the shelf so it is 'ready for the next person'.

Objects such as drinking cups and glasses, plates and bowls, vases and basins are made of china and glass. This not only makes them more appealing, but also means they are breakable. Many of the sets of materials include tiny objects, such as beads or small cubes. The fact so many objects are breakable, or so easy to lose, encourages children to take more care. If materials are broken or incomplete, they are removed from the shelves immediately, and will not be available for the children to use again until they can be returned to the shelf in perfect condition.

Children often choose to work with a material on the floor. To mark out a workspace on the floor, children fetch a small, rolled-up rug, or mat. They carefully unroll the mat on the floor, before fetching and laying out the materials on the mat. When they have finished work and returned the materials to the shelf, they carefully roll up the mat again and return it to its storage area.

The Montessori materials are sometimes described as a kind of 'magic key' children use to unlock the culture around them and to make it their own (Montessori, 1912/1964: 239). The order in which the materials are placed on the shelves reflects the order in which they are typically presented to the children to create 'a world of progressive interest' (Montessori, 1949/1982: 181).

Lessons

Montessori educators give lessons to show children how to act in the environment and how to use the materials. The lessons, often called presentations by Montessori educators, are mostly given to individual children, and sometimes to small groups. Whole-group lessons are rare in the Children's House and are most common in new classrooms when teachers are establishing basic routines. A Montessori lesson contributes to children's freedom by giving them a 'model' of how to work with the learning materials and of what can be achieved with practice. Learning takes place when children work with the material independently.

Children are free to choose an activity once they have had a lesson, in other words, when they know how to do the activity. Thus, as a child gains more knowledge, the child also gains more freedom.

Preparing a Montessori environment for an Infant Community

The newborn's first environment is the home. In the first weeks of life the attachment forged when the baby is cuddled and fed, and the love the baby receives from parents and carers, builds the bedrock of trust and security on which the child's entire future rests. Montessori Assistants to Infancy offer parents many ideas for establishing order and routine within the home, for giving the infant as much freedom of movement and independence as possible, and for setting up everyday activities so the infant can join in and contribute. A little one venturing away from home for the first time can attend one of two Montessori environments prepared for infants under the age of three.

• For babies of working parents, there is the Nido, or nest, a nurturing Montessori day care environment for children from 2 to 12 months.
• Once children are walking, they can join a Montessori Infant Community for children aged from one to three years.

The Nido and Infant Community environments are not the same as the more familiar day care or playgroup environment. Like the Children's House, a Montessori environment for infants is a world in miniature, this time to the scale of even smaller children, and, like the Children's House, it is designed to give these very young children interesting activities and as much freedom and independence as possible.

Like all Montessori environments, the Infant Community environment is light and airy, clean and safe, ordered and beautiful, with plenty of space for children to move about freely. Because babies and toddlers use their senses to explore the environment, there is a variety of surfaces, for example, tiles, wood, glass and fabric. Fabrics used for soft furnishings, such as rugs, quilts, pillows and cushions, are chosen for their sensory appeal as well as for safety and practicality. There are wall mirrors at the children's height and striking mobiles that catch the eye. Furniture and objects are real, and matched to the size of the children and to their strength and abilities. To build equilibrium and gross motor skills, there are stairs to climb and objects to grasp and move. To contribute to the order, there is a designated space for each activity, whether it is food preparation, eating or nappy changing.

All activities are pre-prepared so these tiny children need as little adult assistance as possible. Floor beds enable children to sleep when they wish, and move about again when they wake up, without needing an adult's help. Parents are encouraged to dress children in clothing they can put on and take off by themselves. Carefully pre-measured portions help children prepare food independently or in collaboration with adults. The emphasis is on allowing the children to reveal what they are capable of doing on their own. For example, if children can walk, they are not carried; if children can stand, they are not forced to lie down when they are changed; if children cannot yet hold a spoon, adults do not force food into their mouths but hold the spoon within reach so they can choose when and how much to eat. The Assistant to Infancy is constantly observing, always ready to adjust the environment to enable each child to find new interests and challenges and to ensure children are not distracted, over-stimulated or overwhelmed.

Preparing a Montessori environment for children aged from six to nine

The order of the Children's House is an external guide for children under the age of six to help them construct an internal order. The order in Montessori classrooms prepared for children older than six is not quite so meticulously protected and micro-managed. Apart from anything else, the children in these classrooms are physically taller and stronger, more robust and sturdy, more socially outgoing, and more lively. Knowing what things are and how to do things no longer satisfies these children. They want to know why, what for and how things come to be the way they are. The gentle 'hum' of the Children's House is replaced with the increased exuberance of the older children. The concern with order and harmony is maintained, however, but now this concern extends way beyond the social, temporal and spatial limits of the classroom.

In the manner of all Montessori classrooms, classrooms for children from six to nine are prepared to give children as much freedom as possible, while maintaining social harmony and the conditions that support learning. There is an emphasis on building ethical as well as practical and intellectual independence. Children are free to move about and to work uninterrupted on self-chosen activities, for as long as they like and with whom they like, but without causing harm or disturbing anyone else's work. These older children often choose to work together collaboratively in pairs or in groups. For this reason, group lessons are more common than in the Children's House.

The Montessori curriculum for children from six to nine is rich and expansive, encompassing studies in language and mathematics, astronomy and geology, history and geography, biology, music and art. Each area of study has its own place in the classroom, with the learning materials sequenced in order of presentation. The classroom is organized to embody a web of interconnected knowledge.

The keys giving children entry into each area of knowledge are the materials, and the lessons the materials generate. Like all Montessori materials, these are beautiful, kept in good condition and designed to capture children's attention and to hold their interest. The materials are often augmented with wall charts and displays related to current topics of interest and research.

Stories, lessons and exercises for this age group are designed to:

• spark the imagination
• exploit their interest in the reasons for things
• generate questions and discussion
• act as starting points for independent exploration and research.

At the same time, because children in this age group are learning to be socially responsible, they are made aware of the standards set by local curriculum authorities, in areas such as arithmetic, reading, spelling and handwriting. The classroom provides a wide variety of opportunities to help children achieve these standards.

Consumables, such as stationery and art materials, and equipment, such as microscopes, computers and musical instruments, are located in accessible places, always available for children to use as they complete their tasks and pursue their interests. The classroom also has a collection of books, comprising both quality children's literature and a small research library of factual books relating to the key topics of the curriculum.

Because children of this age are eager to explore beyond the classroom, they are shown how to organize their own visits to places relevant to their current interests and research topics, for example, a specialist library or botanical garden, a factory or farm, a planetarium, art gallery or museum. The goal is for children to learn how to find the place they want to visit on a map, its opening and closing times, how to travel there by public transport, how long the trip takes and how much it costs. Preparation for a trip might include using the telephone to make a booking or to ask an adult to accompany them. In recent years, of course, the Internet has become another means for children to explore beyond the classroom walls.

Activity

In Montessori prepared environments, children are surrounded by a selection of alluring objects; they are free to move around, to choose their own activity and workspace, and to work with their chosen activity in their chosen space for as long as they like. We have seen how this template is adapted in Montessori schools to meet the needs of three different age groups:

- infants and toddlers from birth to three years
- preschool children aged from three to six years
- children aged from six to nine years in the early years of school.

Observe early childhood settings for each of these age groups. Use the following questions to evaluate, from the Montessori perspective, the preparation of each setting.

1. Describe the appearance of the spaces in which children work and play. Is there enough light? Is there an outdoor area accessible to the children? Can children move around easily and safely? Is everything clean and well ordered? Are consumables, such as paper, pencils and glue, replenished every day? Is it clear where everything belongs so children can fetch and put things away independently?
2. How is the setting prepared to meet the children's interests and needs? Does it invite purposeful, focused activity?
3. How many adults are in the room? What are their roles? Do they treat the children with respect and enable them to be independent? How do the adults give lessons and show children how to do things? In what other ways do the adults interact with the children?
4. How are children grouped in the space? How do they interact socially?
5. What freedoms do children have? What limits are placed on these freedoms?
6. Identify the different areas in the setting. What is the function of each area? Would the differences in function from one area to the next be obvious to children? Are there ways each area could be made more attractive, more accessible and more functional from a child's perspective?
7. Describe the objects, learning materials and activities offered to children. Are they enticing and interesting for children of this age? Do they hold the children's attention? Are the materials in good condition? Are they stored so children can distinguish one set of materials from another?
8. Is each set of learning materials unique, with a distinct purpose and use of its own? Do children understand how to use each set of materials? Do the children respect the materials and look forward to using them? To what degree are children free to choose their own learning materials and activities?

Use this evaluation to think about how the setting might be enhanced using what you know about the Montessori 'prepared environment'.

Movement and the mind

We have seen that Montessori educators interpret a child's freely chosen, spontaneous activity as the child's work. This work always involves movement of some kind. Human movement, in the Montessori view, is an expression of the human mind.

Freedom, purposeful movement and concentration in early childhood

Dr Montessori compared the development of movement in human children with that of young animals. When young animals, such as cats or horses, are born, they quickly, sometimes almost immediately, approximate the coordination and agility of the adults of the species. Newborn babies, in contrast, have none of the balance, coordination and dexterity of adult humans. During their extended infancy, human children must gain control of movement. This involves effort and repetitive practice in which children exert themselves both physically and mentally at the same time. In the preschool years children make this effort because they find movements such as the following so interesting:

- carrying, climbing and balancing, in other words, in moving the whole body with equilibrium
- taking part independently in the everyday activities of the social life they see around them
- using the hand with exactness and precision.

Dr Montessori observed that, when children engage in freely chosen activity directed towards a goal, mental effort and physical effort become coordinated and focused. Over time, if children regularly use their minds to direct their movement, they develop the ability to control, voluntarily and independently, both their movements and thoughts. In other words, as they gain control of their muscles, they gain control of their minds. Children who can control their minds are able to focus their attention, voluntarily, for extended periods, that is, they have the ability to concentrate. In Montessori terms, this is how they liberate themselves from being slaves to their own impulses.

The more children are able to bring their movements and attention under voluntary control, in other words, the more they are able to direct and regulate themselves, the less they need to be directed and regulated by others, and the more free and independent they become. Children take the first step on this developmental pathway when they choose activities they find intrinsically interesting, that is, activities matched to the sensitive periods of their age. Once on the pathway children are led by the activity towards self-regulation, concentration and freedom. This pathway is represented in Figure 3.1.

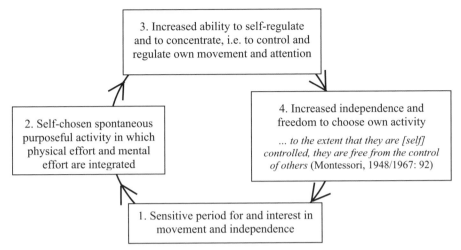

Figure 3.1   The pathway to self-regulation, concentration and freedom

Activity

Observe children's activity in an early childhood setting. Look for examples of each of the following:

- an activity which Montessori educators would call work
- free, unstructured and undirected activity.

For each example, answer the following questions:

- How does the activity aid the child's development?
- Does this type of activity contribute to the development of concentration and independence? If yes, how? If not, why not?

Two types of movement: balancing the body and using the hand

Human movement is described in the Montessori tradition as developing along two separate, but related, lines:

- 'walking and keeping one's balance'
- 'the development of the hand' (Montessori, 1949/1982: 132).

The sensitive period for movement propels infants towards crucial developmental milestones – grasping objects, rolling over, sitting up, crawling and walking. None of these milestones is achieved automatically; each requires effort. Observing young children as they work to achieve each milestone reveals just how much effort is involved.

Once infants are walking, the power of the sensitive period for movement continues to hold sway. Toddlers and young children cannot resist climbing, swinging from bars, carrying things and walking with care along edges, cracks and raised narrow ridges, in other words, using every opportunity to practise and perfect coordination and balance. They also have a strong desire to move in ways that build strength, including:

• carrying heavy things
• walking for long distances
• finding exceptionally challenging ways to climb.

Such activities sometimes cause adults concern. The task for adults is to create opportunities for children to do these things in ways that are interesting, challenging and safe.

At the same time, the heightened interest children have in tiny things from about the age of two propels them to extend the use of their hands beyond grasping. As small children try to pick up the tiny things they find so beguiling, they learn to use, with increasing precision, the thumb and forefinger in a pincer grip. In other words, they learn to use their hands in a uniquely human way. From this universal starting point during early childhood, humans over time have developed an infinite number of ways to work with their hands. 'It is thanks to the hand, the companion of the mind', wrote Dr Montessori (1949/1982: 131), 'that civilization has arisen'. In order to direct, control and perfect all these movements, human children must focus their minds and concentrate.

Purposeful movement, in the Montessori view, underpins the social life of humans. It is because Montessori early childhood environments are prepared to include opportunities for interesting, purposeful activity within an ordered social setting that children in these environments can be given the freedom Montessori educators believe is essential for their optimal development.

Reflection point 〰

When next you see a small child trying hard to walk along the line between paving stones, to pick up a tiny shiny pebble, or to imitate the action of an adult or older child, observe closely, without disturbing, and you will see the child concentrating, that is, integrating both mental and physical powers. What you are observing is human development in progress.

Activity

When you observe a child concentrating to achieve a goal, use the following guidelines to record the interwoven development of movement and mind.

- Record the child's age and stage of development.
- Record what it was that attracted the child's interest and initiated the activity in the first place.
- Describe the child's movements. How well does the child walk and maintain balance? What hand movements does the child use? Does the child use the palm to grasp objects, or is the child learning to use the finger–thumb pincer grip?
- How much effort, both physical and mental, does the activity require? Is the child working at the limit of his or her strength and concentration? How can you tell?
- How long does the child concentrate on the activity? Does the child repeat any elements of the activity?
- Does the child achieve the goal in the end? How does that make the child feel? How can you tell?
- How do you think this activity has contributed to the child's development, both physical and mental?

Incorporating a range of movement into children's activity

Ideally, playgrounds and other environments for young children designed to encourage a range of movement should not only be safe, but also interesting and challenging. This can be difficult, especially if those environments are to meet stringent safety standards of local authorities. A playground designed to accommodate the full range of movement identified by Dr Montessori would include opportunities for children to do the following activities:

Movement of the whole body
- rolling, crawling and sliding (e.g. down slopes, through tunnels)
- climbing
- swinging (both seated and by the arms)
- holding and carrying
- balancing (e.g. along narrow raised ridges)
- walking (on different surfaces and gradients, up and down stairs).

Movement of the hand
- grasping and manipulating objects
- using the thumb and forefinger pincer grip.

In such a playground young children would find many possibilities for coordinating physical and mental effort to exercise and gain control of both muscles and mind.

From attention deficit to attention in abundance

During the time between birth and starting school children are expected to develop the ability to concentrate, at least long enough to understand instructions and to participate in school activities. Children who do not learn to concentrate successfully, who never seem able to focus their attention, are often labelled as having an attention deficit. A great deal has been written about attention deficit in children, about its diagnosis and treatment. There is far less information, however, about how children learn to pay attention and to concentrate in the first place. How might early childhood educators help children to have attention in abundance rather than in deficit?

According to Montessori educators, if the environment of a young child, especially before the age of six, is made up largely of visual material, even of good quality, the child's attention tends to slip quickly from one thing to the next. Moving images on screens, on the other hand, tend to mesmerize young children, controlling their attention by external means. In the Montessori view, small children focus their attention most effectively when they are manipulating real, concrete objects in purposeful ways that require concentration. Importantly, during this type of activity they are making their own decisions. With each conscious, goal-directed choice, they are learning to control their attention by themselves.

The ability to concentrate is nurtured, in the Montessori tradition, when a young child is engaged in activity under the following conditions:

- The child is interested in the activity and chose to do it.
- The activity is purposeful, requiring physical movement directed by mental effort.
- The child manipulates concrete objects to achieve the goal.
- The child has been shown, very precisely, what the goal is, the steps needed to achieve the goal and ways to self-correct if needed.
- The child is free to repeat the activity for as long as he or she wishes at his or her own pace.
- The child is not interrupted, no matter whether the motivation for interruption is to praise, to assist or to correct.

Young children's activity under these conditions is called work by Montessori educators. The more time children spend working in this way, the more abundant is the attention under their control. In order to extend the powers of concentration in children over the age of six, Montessori educators say these conditions need to be broadened to take advantage of the intense interest older children have in:

- discovering the reasons for things
- working collaboratively in a group
- exploring ethical issues.

Developing intellectual and ethical independence after the age of six

In the Montessori tradition, the years from three to six when children are working in the Children's House are the years when purposeful activity involving exact use of the hand is of intense interest, and has, therefore, the greatest potential for fixing the child's attention and for building concentration. After the age of six children become intensely interested in the reasons for things. Looking for reasons becomes the new focus of their attention and the new starting point for the cycles of integrated mental and physical activity that build concentration and, ultimately, intellectual independence.

The ability to self-regulate developed in the Children's House becomes, in Montessori classrooms for six- to nine-year-olds, the basis for ethical independence. Children now want to be part of a peer group, and they begin to look outward to their social group as a further source of regulation. When playing together, they will often spend as much time devising and discussing the rules of a game as they spend playing the game itself. They concentrate hard in order to keep to the rules they have worked out together, and intense discussions can result when there is disagreement about how to interpret the rules. The Montessori environment for these children is prepared to help them build independently a community in which the rules for maintaining social harmony are worked out collectively. In this way, children learn not only social independence, but also social responsibility. Freedom for children over the age of six, therefore, includes the freedom to look for the reasons for things and to contribute to rules for maintaining the harmony of the classroom, as well as the freedom to explore the inevitable ethical issues that arise.

Adults who spend time with six- and seven-year-old children are very familiar with the tendency of these children to 'tell' what another child has done in the hope that the adult will make a judgement and determine a consequence. This happens most often when children feel that a rule has been contravened. Adults tend to interpret this behaviour as 'telling tales'. Montessori educators, in contrast, view this behaviour as an expression of a sensitive period for investigating ethics. The features of this sensitive period are a heightened interest in:

• the difference between right and wrong
• what the wider society considers to be just and ethical behaviour
• the consequences that should follow if socially agreed rules are broken.

A child who 'tells tales' is, thus, conducting research. For this reason, when children in Montessori classrooms 'tell tales', or find themselves involved in conflict about how to keep the rules, the issues are treated as interesting ethical questions to be explored from all perspectives. Children are encouraged to come up with solutions that benefit everyone.

Limits to freedom

In Montessori classrooms children are not free to do what they like, for example, to be disruptive, aggressive or disorderly. If children are unable to control their own movements and are at the mercy of their involuntary impulses, in the Montessori tradition, they are not yet free. Montessori educators intervene in such behaviour, distancing the child from the source of the problem and providing the child with the control they are unable to provide for themselves. Often they will guide the child towards something they know from observation will capture the child's interest and attention, even if, at first, that interest and attention are only fleeting.

Once a child shows interest in something and begins to concentrate, the child is not interrupted. Montessori educators neither correct nor praise concentrating children, nor do they hurry them. Later, when the child's activity is completed, in the child's own time, the adult might acknowledge how much the child appeared to enjoy the work, but neither the work, nor the child, will be evaluated.

If a child's behaviour reveals a lack of knowledge or skill, the teacher will give a lesson, usually on another day so the child does not become self-conscious. Children are given lessons to show them how to move, both themselves and the objects in the room, to prevent disturbance or breakages. When disturbance or breakages occur, children are shown how to manage the consequences, for example, how to apologize or how to clean up.

Montessori educators also believe that, once a child is able to complete an activity independently, an adult who keeps on helping and interrupting becomes an obstacle to the child's development, as, for example, when an adult:

• carries a two-year-old who can walk
• interrupts a four-year-old dressing herself in order to praise her for doing it well
• intervenes in a disagreement between seven-year-olds when they can solve the problem for themselves.

Case study 📁

In a Montessori Children's House, a group of children had set the table for lunch. A special place had been set for each child. Amy wanted to sit in someone else's place. This caused distress both to the child whose place she wanted and to the child whom she didn't want to sit beside. The teacher quietly took Amy aside and gave her the choice of sitting in her own place or at another place where no one else was already sitting. The teacher left Amy alone to make her decision in her own time, telling her to sit in whichever of those two places she chose whenever she was ready.

Reflection point 〰️

Allowing children to choose from a limited number of possible alternatives to disruptive or distressing behaviour is a strategy often used by Montessori teachers. Whichever choice the child makes is respected and supported. The need to make a decision tends to capture the child's attention. The disruptive or distressing behaviour is not an available choice.

Summary ☐

This chapter has described the environments prepared by Montessori educators for three multi-age early childhood settings. The purpose of these settings is to give children as much freedom as possible and to match children with activities that interest them. These activities are purposeful and involve concrete objects and movement, particularly of the hand. When children focus their attention on the precise movements of their hands needed to achieve a goal, they learn to concentrate. If children are free to choose and persevere with purposeful activities they find interesting, activities that combine mental and physical effort, they gradually learn to regulate themselves.

Things to think about

Recall a familiar example of each of the following early childhood settings:

- a baby at home with a parent and a toddler sibling
- a day care centre for babies and toddlers
- a playgroup for toddlers
- a nursery, kindergarten or preschool classroom
- a classroom of children in their first years at school.

Review each setting using the following questions:

1. What were the children free to do? What limits were placed on their freedom?
2. For what proportion of their time were the children free to choose their own activity?
3. When children were given freedom to choose their own activity, how was the children's safety and well-being taken into account?
4. When the children are given complete freedom, what happened? When limits are placed on children's freedom, what happened? Why?
5. In what ways does the setting support or work against the development of concentration?
6. How would you adjust the environment in each case to give children maximum freedom and to enhance the development of concentration?

What have your studies and experience in early childhood education so far told you about helping young children to develop concentration and control attention? How does this accord with the Montessori approach to the development of concentration in early childhood? How adaptable do you think the Montessori approach is to early childhood settings in general?

4

The exercises of practical life

Chapter objectives

- To introduce the first of the two foundation areas of the Montessori curriculum, the exercises of practical life.
- To consider the exercises of practical life as a means of refining motor control, regulating attention and developing self-confidence.
- To explore the role of imitation and repetition in the practical life exercises.
- To provide an overview of different types of practical life exercises for children at different stages of development.

Movement directed by the mind is the means by which children learn to regulate their attention and to concentrate in Montessori classrooms. Children first learn to concentrate in Montessori classrooms during the exercises of practical life. These exercises, according to Montessori educators, help children learn to make voluntary choices, not controlled by impulse, but by their own willpower. To have willpower means to have enough self-control to persist until a goal, even a challenging one, is achieved. In other words, willpower weaves together:

- interest in achieving a goal
- choosing and carrying out the actions needed to achieve the goal
- persisting until the goal is achieved.

In Dr Montessori's time some people believed that to socialize children it was necessary to 'break their will', but she argued that this was irrational.

Children are not born with willpower, so instead of trying to break something they do not yet have, we should help them build it up for themselves (Montessori, 1912/1964: 366).

What are the exercises of practical life and what is their purpose?

The exercises of practical life are based on the ways people in the culture relate to each other socially, as well as the ways in which they complete everyday tasks. In each exercise a single social skill or practical purpose is isolated and brought to the child's attention. The exercises are real-life activities using, not toys, but fully functional objects matched to the size of a child's hand and strength. The exercises of practical life have the same status in the classroom as activities in which children learn educational knowledge, such as mathematics or reading. They provide children with endless opportunities to imitate the everyday behaviours of people in their social group, and to repeat these behaviours as often as they like. In the process, according to Montessori educators, children gain independence, develop concentration and build willpower.

When young children struggle with an item of clothing, or drop food on the floor when eating, the problem is easily solved if adults simply take over. This approach, however, is not the Montessori way. Instead, young children are taught to do everyday tasks for themselves. This is the purpose of the exercises of practical life, which provide children with the knowledge and skills they need to be independent members of the classroom community, and to contribute to everyday life at home.

Because these exercises are based on the everyday customs and domestic routines of the child's community, they link Montessori classrooms to the children's homes and culture. Each successfully learned practical life exercise gives children more freedom and more choice at home and at school. The exercises of practical life also help children develop control and coordination of their movements, both whole-body (gross motor) and hand (fine motor) movements.

The indirect, but fundamentally important, purpose of the exercises of practical life is to give children culturally appropriate and relevant ways of using the mind to regulate movement and attention. In Montessori classrooms being in command of one's own movements and attention becomes the foundation on which later educational progress is built.

Imitation and repetition

Young children love to do things for themselves and to do what adults and older children do. They are very interested in everyday social customs and they want to be included, in meaningful and independent ways, in the activities of social life they see around them every day. Children's interest in imitating and repeating everyday activities is exploited in the exercises of practical life.

When Montessori teachers show children how to do practical life exercises, they apply the principle that 'every useless help is an obstacle to development' (Montessori, 1946: 59–60). The teacher uses precise and economical gestures and language, to show children the objects needed for each exercise and the sequence of their use. No unnecessary, irrelevant or distracting movements or language are used. When a step critical to the success of the activity is reached, the teacher might hesitate or use exaggerated gestures to indicate that this step is a point of interest. For example, the teacher might pause dramatically just before a liquid being poured tips over the lip of the jug, or use an exaggerated gesture to indicate a coloured line on a container that shows the child when to stop pouring.

After the initial presentation, children are free to work with the exercise whenever they want. When they choose to work with it, they imitate the teacher's sequence of movements in order to achieve the goal, for example, a polished mirror or a swept floor. This imitation is never a forced, nor a slavish copying of the teacher, but a consequence of the child's interest. Whenever this interest is ignited, and the child spontaneously chooses to do the exercise, the sequence of movements becomes the child's own, both to practise and to achieve a real purpose in the environment.

Younger children love to repeat self-chosen exercises over and over again, even after the apparent goal of the exercise has been achieved. For example, the mirror might be gleaming, all the dirt on the floor swept up and in the bin, but the child continues to polish or to sweep. This repetition often extends way beyond the limits of an adult's understanding or patience. In a Montessori setting, however, children are free to repeat exercises for as long as they want.

Case study 📁

Ella is three years old and newly arrived in the Children's House. The teacher observes her folding a cloth, shaking it out and folding it over and over again. After ten repetitions the teacher stops counting. Eventually Ella returns the cloth to its place on the shelf. She wanders around the class for a while, very satisfied and happy, before she chooses another activity.

Montessori educators believe it is very important not to interrupt cycles of repetitive activity, because it is through repetition that the young child gains independent control of both movement and attention. Children who are rarely able to complete these cycles of repetitive activity in response to sensitive periods can become either frustrated or passive, in other words, immobilized and inactive, limiting their opportunities to exercise their bodies and their minds.

As children repeat a practical life exercise independently, the material itself reveals errors of control or sequence. For example, a child knows there has been an error when a glass drops or breaks, liquid or rice is spilt, when a chair bangs or scrapes along the floor, or when the goal of the exercise is not achieved. Such errors are opportunities for further teaching and further interaction.

Case study 📁

On our visit to a Children's House in Chapter 2, we saw a box of beads drop when a younger child bumped into an older child. The teacher's response was to observe, without intervening. The older child began to pick up the beads one by one, using her thumb and forefinger in a pincer grip and placing each one back in the box. The younger child also began to pick up the beads. This work continued until all the beads were back in the box.

The children's solution to the problem is an exercise of practical life. The younger child imitates the way the older child picks up the beads, repeating the movement over and over again until all the beads are back in the box. By the end of the work the younger child, through her own physical effort and mental concentration, has regained her equilibrium, both physical and emotional. Learning that she can resolve problems on her own in this way, builds the child's confidence and resilience.

The stages of a practical life lesson

Each exercise of practical life is made up of three stages. This three-stage pattern is found in almost all Montessori exercises.

The three stages of a practical life exercise are:

• the teacher's presentation of the exercise, usually to an individual child
• the child's independent work
• the child's use of the knowledge in another context.

The teacher's presentation

The first stage of a Montessori exercise is the teacher's presentation. The teacher introduces the exercise by telling the child its name and purpose and showing the child where to find the materials, how to carry them to a workspace and how to lay them out ready to start.

The teacher demonstrates how to do the activity, step by step. The sequence of steps is choreographed and rehearsed by the teacher beforehand. Each movement is well defined, very slow and clearly distinguishable from the next so the child can see exactly how it is executed.

While presenting the exercise, the teacher's attention focuses, not on the child, but on the activity, in this way modelling to the child where attention needs to be directed for the exercise to be successful. As the presentation unfolds, the teacher draws the child's attention to points of interest, moments of challenge in the sequence that are critical to achieving the goal of the exercise.

In the Children's House the teacher presents a sequence of steps, then invites the child to try. For very young children, for example, toddlers, the teacher presents one step and then invites the child to try that step, before presenting the next step. If the child loses interest after one step and walks off, the teacher packs the materials away and shows the child more steps on subsequent days.

When rehearsing a practical life exercise before giving a lesson, Montessori teachers often try the exercise with their non-dominant hand so they know how a child doing it for the first time might feel. During presentations, teachers use their dominant hand, but make adjustments for children whose handedness is different from their own.

Activity

Try the following everyday activities using your non-dominant hand:

- washing a surface
- opening a door
- tying a shoelace
- buttoning a shirt
- pouring a drink.

How did you feel? Did you have to concentrate? How much longer than usual did it take to finish the activity? Which parts of the activity proved particularly difficult? What have you learned from this experience that you can apply to your work with young children?

Independent work

The second stage of the exercise occurs when the child chooses the activity and independently imitates and repeats the steps presented by the teacher. This is the stage in which, Montessori educators believe, learning takes place. The practical purpose of the exercise may spark a child's initial interest but the interest is sustained by the sequence of exact and precise movements. Interest drives children's repetition of an exercise, sometimes long after the practical purpose is achieved. During independent work many children talk to themselves as they concentrate on performing each step in the sequence. This self-talk contributes to the 'hum' so often commented upon by first-time visitors to a Montessori Children's House.

The child's desire to choose the exercise is a reflection of how well the teacher has matched the activity to the child's interests. If a child shows no interest in following up a presentation with independent work, the teacher continues to observe the child's spontaneous activity and presents other exercises that might be better matched to the child's current interests. How well an exercise has been pre-analysed, prepared and presented contributes to the child's ability to complete it successfully.

The teacher observes each child's independent work and might give a follow-up presentation at a later time to show how to refine some element of the exercise. If children are not successful at all, the teacher will redirect their attention to an activity they can complete successfully. The teacher might repeat the lesson at a later time, but always in a way that ensures the child has no sense of ever having been unsuccessful.

Using the knowledge in another context

The success of the first and second stages of a practical life exercise is demonstrated by the third stage. At this stage the know-how gained through the exercise has been added to the child's repertoire of automated, everyday routines, for example, when a child without prompting washes the table after an art activity. The teacher's task is to prepare the environment so children have as many opportunities as possible to move into this stage.

Montessori educators believe that the everyday know-how children gain through the exercises of practical life is a solid foundation for self-confidence. Because children become genuinely competent and accomplished in the tasks of daily life, their self-confidence is built on a reality they can verify for themselves every day.

A sample lesson: washing tables

Table washing is a popular practical life exercise in most Montessori classrooms. It is first presented to toddlers in the Infant Community, one step at a time. By the time children are in the classroom for six- to nine-year-olds, washing the table is an automatic part of the clean up after eating, art, science or cooking.

In the Children's House washing a table combines vigorous movement with water play in a sequence of precise movements. The whole exercise demands quite sophisticated levels of fine motor control, and concentration, if the child is to complete the task successfully. A version of table washing which is common in many Children's Houses is outlined in Table 4.1.

If a child wants to do the activity but is not ready for all four sequences, a simplified version can be presented. The exercise can also be made more challenging for older children.

After several repetitions children start to memorise the whole series until they can wash tables independently in any context. As they do the steps, children practise movements and directionality that later become the basis for handwriting.

Types of practical life exercises

Table washing is a practical life exercise children learn so they can contribute to the care of the environment at school and at home. In the Children's House there are the five types of practical life exercise:

• lessons in grace and courtesy

- preliminary exercises
- care of yourself
- care of the environment
- whole body movement.

Lessons in grace and courtesy

The lessons in grace and courtesy are a feature of the Children's House. They match the interest young children have in learning the social customs of the family and community with whom they live. Knowing how to interact with others with grace and courtesy is, in the Montessori tradition, another area of knowledge for children to learn, just like, for example, mathematics. Children are offered knowledge about grace and courtesy as a guide, not to force them to behave in certain ways, but to give them choices about what to do in different social situations. Challenging behaviour is often the result of feeling left out and not knowing what to do. Having knowledge about what to do in different social situations, and about how to resolve social problems, builds confidence and resilience.

Table 4.1 Table washing: the teacher's presentation in the Children's House

Opening phase	The teacher opens the presentation by: • establishing a need for the activity (a dirty table) and inviting, through gesture and language, the child to respond • indicating the location of the table washing set on the practical life shelf carrying the set to the table • setting up the objects in an array • putting on apron, fetching and pouring water
The series of activity sequences	The teacher presents the following sequence of movements, indicating points of interest: • dampen the table, using a sponge in parallel vertical strokes from left to right • apply the soap to the brush and scrub the table, using a brush in rows of anticlockwise circular movements from left to right, large circles on the table top and small ones around the edges • rinse the table, using a sponge in parallel vertical strokes from left to right • dry the table, using a cloth in rows of anticlockwise circular movements from left to right, large circles on the table top and small ones around the edges The teacher offers the child a turn, that is, an opportunity to imitate, at appropriate moments. At the end the teacher invites the child to do the whole activity.
Closing phase	When the child is ready to finish, the teacher closes the presentation by showing the child how to: • clean up • return objects to their array • put the objects away.

The lessons in grace and courtesy show children how to manage social relations in the classroom and beyond. The lessons are presented in short and charming role-plays. They show children how to interact with other people respectfully and with empathy, and how to move and use language so their actions and interactions maintain the order and harmony of the environment. A teacher, or a more expert child, acts out movements and language, and the children imitate. Children usually love this dramatic play, and so they think learning about grace and courtesy is fun. This contrasts with the common childhood experience of only finding out what should have been done when an adult very publicly draws attention to a social misdemeanour.

When, for example, a child's loud movements disturb others, a Montessori teacher will redirect the child's attention to an activity the teacher knows will capture the child's interest. At a later time the teacher might include the child in a small group grace and courtesy lesson that shows everyone in the group how to walk in the room without disturbing anyone. The child to whom the lesson is directed is not singled out or made to feel he or she has done something wrong.

When establishing a new class, and at the beginning of a new year, Montessori teachers make a list of the lessons in grace and courtesy children will need if they are to build harmonious social relations with each other and with their teachers. The lessons vary according to the age of the children and the local culture.

A typical list of grace and courtesy lessons for the Children's House is found in Table 4.2. The lessons are organized according to whether they are based on movement or on language.

Table 4.2 Grace and courtesy

Lessons in grace and courtesy	
Movement	*Language*
• shake hands	• listen
• let someone pass, for example, in a small passage way	• greet or take leave of someone
• carry and offer sharp objects	• introduce yourself or someone else
• fetch a chair for visitor	• invite someone in
• cough	• interrupt
• hold a door open for someone	• apologise
	• make an offer or a request
	• say please and thank you
	• answer the telephone
	• buy something in a shop

Case study 📁

Josh has just returned to the Children's House after an extended absence. The teacher interprets his rowdy, disruptive behaviour as a way of managing many recent changes in his life. Josh had chosen table washing, after he had been shown how, as his first work every morning that week. The Montessori table washing activity tends to hold the interest of children a little younger than Josh, so the teacher hopes to extend his interest by setting up an opportunity for him, on the morning of our visit, to use his knowledge to contribute, in a real way, to the care of the environment.

Focusing his attention on this activity, and persisting until the task is finished, helps Josh to:

- regain control of himself and his attention
- refine the precision of his movement
- rebuild his sense of belonging within the classroom community.

A morning will soon come when Josh chooses a different first work, but this is Josh's decision to make when he is ready.

It is only after Josh has regained his equilibrium through his own activity, that the teacher, without commenting on his disorderly arrival, includes him in a lesson showing a small group of children how to put their things away. She gives Josh extra responsibility in the lesson, both because he is older than the others in the group and to reinforce his sense of belonging.

Activity 🔲

1. Observe how children are taught culturally appropriate ways of behaving in an early childhood setting and consider the advantages and disadvantages of this approach.
2. Create a grace and courtesy role-play that will interest and charm the children in this setting. After practising the role-play several times, deliver the lesson to a small group of children. Record what you observe. How are these lessons the same as, and how are they different from, dramatic play?

The preliminary exercises

When toddlers in a Montessori Infant Community want to hang up a wet cloth, for example, they are shown how to use a peg. In other words, toddlers are taught movements at the point of need. In the Children's House, in contrast, preliminary exercises show children basic movements before they need to use them in more elaborate practical life exercises. Through preliminary exercises children learn:

- whole body coordination and equilibrium
- more refined movement of the hand, especially the thumb and forefinger pincer grip.

They also learn spatial awareness, for example, how to avoid bumping into people and things and how to work within the limits of a mat on a table or floor.

A typical list of preliminary lessons for the Children's House is found in Table 4.3. The lessons are organized according to whether they involve whole body movement or movement of the hand.

Table 4.3   Preliminary exercises in the Children's House

Preliminary exercises	
Whole body	*Hand*
• walking in the classroom without disturbing others • opening and closing a door • carrying a chair, sitting on a chair and pushing in a chair • carrying floor mats, trays and containers • rolling and unrolling floor mats	• folding cloths • spooning rice or beans • using pegs • pouring rice or water • opening and closing containers

As children learn to control their hand movements with increasing precision, they are introduced to practical life exercises in which the preliminary movements are combined into the more complex sequences. The dexterity gained in the preliminary exercises is also exploited in manual and creative arts, for example, cooking, sewing, stringing beads, weaving, knitting, clay modelling, woodwork and model making.

Extensions of the preliminary exercises include two very distinctive Montessori activities:

- walking on the line
- the exercise of silence.

In every Montessori Children's House, in an open space, there is a line marked out on the floor. The line is like a tightrope stretched into the shape of an ellipse. In response to a musical cue children 'balance' on the line, placing their feet carefully heel to toe. This requires a great deal of effort for children whose walking is still maturing. Once children have mastered the walking movement, the exercise becomes a very peaceful, contemplative one.

When children are ready, they make the balancing more challenging by choosing objects to carry. Popular objects carried on the line include one or more flags (to look at instead of their feet), a bell (so it makes no sound), a glass of water (so it does not spill) and a tray of objects (keeping the objects perfectly still). Extensions of the walking on the line exercise for older children include moving on the line in response to changes in the rhythm and tempo of the music. As well as developing equilibrium and coordination, the walking on the line exercises prepare for dance and physical education.

In every Montessori environment there is a signal that means everyone in the room stops what they are doing, remains still and listens. This signal might be a tinkling bell, the soft sound of a gong or notes played on a musical instrument. To respond to this signal, children must inhibit their movement. One day, in the first Children's House, when a visitor arrived with a tiny, sleeping baby, Dr Montessori discovered how much young children love to inhibit their movement. She asked the children how quiet they could be so the baby would not be disturbed, and the children became completely silent. To her surprise, Dr Montessori observed how much the children enjoyed making this silence. This is the origin of the Montessori exercise of silence.

The exercise of silence is introduced after children have had a lot of practice with the preliminary exercises and the exercises in grace and courtesy, and when the teacher is sure the children who are going to participate can succeed in a cooperative game of this kind. On an agreed signal, perhaps a sign with the word 'Silence' written on it, a dimming of the lights or a quiet word from the teacher, the children sit together in silence. The teacher sits just out of sight by the door with a list of the children's names. The teacher calls each child's name very softly one by one, leaving until last, children with the most control. As children hear their name, they walk as quietly as they can out to the teacher. The extended silence, and the control and cooperation it demands from everyone, can make this game seem quite magical.

Caring for yourself

In Montessori classrooms children are given practical life lessons that show them how to look after themselves. These lessons are matched to children's needs, interests and levels of fine motor control. They can be traced back, in the Montessori tradition, to a lesson Dr Montessori gave in the first Children's House. The street children at the school often had runny noses, so she gathered the children into a group and acted out, in precise detail, all the steps the children needed to follow to blow their noses hygienically and courteously. For the lesson Dr Montessori selected a perfectly laundered, embroidered, white handkerchief. The beautiful handkerchief and Dr Montessori's slow, and theatrical, movements, punctuated by slightly exaggerated pauses, captivated the children. When she finished, they applauded.

A typical list of lessons for showing children how to care for themselves is found in Table 4.4. Lessons in this series relate to food preparation, dressing and personal care.

Table 4.4 Self-care exercises

Self-care exercises		
Food preparation	*Dressing*	*Personal care*
• pour a drink • cut up fruit	• clean shoes • put on a coat	• wash hands • comb hair

Food preparation in the Infant Community

Toddlers are very interested in food, so food preparation is a feature of Montessori Infant Communities. These tiny children often, for example, prepare bread dough. All the ingredients are pre-measured in exact amounts and placed in separate containers. One step at a time, the children are shown how to mix the ingredients together, and how to knead and shape the dough. Then the dough is carefully wrapped in a cloth and the children take it home to bake in the oven and share with their families. Infant Communities have been known to prepare pizza, pasta and even Christmas plum puddings in the same way.

Dressing frames in the Children's House

A Montessori Children's House always has a set of dressing frames. These are wooden frames to which are attached two pieces of matching fabric. The two pieces of fabric on each frame can be fastened, each frame using a different type of fastening. Children practise the dressing frame fastenings they need to master in order to be able to dress and undress themselves. Dressing frames include those that show children how to use buttons, snap fasteners, hooks and eyes, buckles and zips, how to tie ribbons into bows, and how to thread laces through eyelets. While most Montessori schools have, at least, a button frame and a bow-tying frame, dressing frames can vary depending on the type of fastenings children at a particular school need to master in order to be able to dress themselves. During their training Montessori teachers spend much time analysing and practising the use of dressing frames. They pride themselves on being able to present, for example, the button frame or the bow-tying frame to a child, with every necessary movement clearly distinguishable and all unnecessary movements eliminated, so that the child has the best chance of success.

Hand washing as meditation

The Montessori exercises in self-care achieve very useful and pragmatic purposes related to independence and hygiene. For example, children learn to dress themselves, to prepare their own food, to pour their own drinks, to clean up and to wash their hands. The exercises can also be very calming, helping children to refocus and regain equilibrium. Where the lessons in grace and courtesy show children how to treat others with respect and care, through these lessons children learn to direct the same level of respect and care towards themselves.

A particularly beautiful, meditative lesson in the Children's House is hand washing. This exercise is in addition to the regular hand washing, perhaps set up with simple equipment at an appropriate sink, where children learn to wash their hands in the bathroom, or before eating or preparing food. The more elaborate hand washing exercise teaches children to respect their hands and to honour the wonderful work these hands do every day.

The hand washing equipment is set up on a special table or stand. Traditionally, an old-fashioned matching glass or ceramic pitcher and bowl are used, accompanied by an embroidered linen hand towel, an attractive nailbrush and special soap and hand cream. There are five sequences of movements:

1. Fetching water in the pitcher and filling the bowl, with attention to water levels as points of interest.
2. Wetting, washing and rinsing the hands, with shaking off excess water, making suds between the palms, and washing palms, tops of hands and each finger as points of interest.
3. Cleaning nails, with shaking off excess water, pulling the nail brush across the soap, brushing under nails and rinsing hands as points of interest.
4. Drying and moisturising hands, with checking between fingers and the hand cream disappearing into the skin as points of interest.

If a simpler exercise is needed, the nail cleaning and moisturising can be left out.

Caring for the environment

Children in Montessori classrooms learn how to contribute to the care of the environment, at school and at home, indoors and outdoors. Table washing, for example, is an exercise in caring for the environment.

Everything needed for each activity is stored together as a set on a tray on a shelf, on hooks or on stands accessible to the children. All the objects in each set are fully functional, no toys are ever used, but the objects match the size and strength of the children who use them. Each set of objects is colour-coded to show they go together. For example, the set of objects used to wash tables might be colour-coded red. The set would include a red bucket, a red soap-holder, a jug with red tape to mark the water level, an apron made of waterproof fabric in a red pattern, a scrubbing brush with a painted red line, red or pink sponges, a red drying cloth, a red waterproof mat and a red tray for storing the objects on the shelf. If the teacher is unable to find red objects, then red ribbon, a red trim or red embroidery can be added to the objects.

Preparing each set of objects is time-consuming. Montessori teachers spend hours looking for just the right object in just the right size and colour, attaching coloured ribbons and tape, or painting or embroidering them to ensure all objects in each set are just right for each exercise. For Montessori teachers this is time well spent. Attention to detail while preparing an exercise pays off once the set of objects is in the classroom and its use has been presented to the children. When the appeal of a set of objects becomes irresistible, and the children know how to do the exercise on their own, children are enticed into the cycles of independent activity that are so fundamental to the Montessori approach.

Flower arranging is popular in all classrooms. In the infant community children use a funnel to pour water into a vase and then put pre-cut flowers into the vase. In the Children's House children often bring their own flowers, or pick them from the garden. Everything needed for flower arranging is collected together on a tray and colour-coded, including vases, scissors, a jug, a sponge, a bucket and a cloth, and children are given a very detailed lesson. When older children have flowers to arrange, they collect the equipment for themselves.

A typical list of exercises for caring for the Children's House environment is found in Table 4.5. They are organized according to whether they are indoor or outdoor exercises.

Practical life in the Montessori classroom for six- to nine-year-olds

Younger children are interested in the practical life exercises for their own sake, often repeating them over and over again. A young child who has just finished washing a table will often start all over again and repeat the exercise several times, even though the table no longer needs washing. After about the age of six, children are more interested in completing the exercise in order to achieve its social goal, for example, in the case of table washing, a clean table for the next person who wants to use it.

Table 4.5 Caring for the environment in the Children's House

Caring for the environment	
Indoors	*Outdoors*
• dust • polish (e.g. wooden tables, glass mirrors and windows) • clean and polish metal (e.g. silver and brass ornaments) • arrange flowers • sweep • clean windows • wash cloths and cutlery • water pot plants • caring for classroom pets	• water plants • rake leaves • make compost • plant seeds • weed garden • cut flowers • sweep path

For these older children lessons in grace and courtesy are often initiated with a role-play of how not to behave in a particular context, followed by the children creating and performing role-plays to demonstrate a better way. Such lessons can be hilarious, while at the same time satisfying the need of these older children to know the reasons for things.

Older children still need to be shown exactly how to do an exercise, and they need opportunities to imitate and repeat. At this age, however, they are not interested in repeating the same thing over and over again, and they lose interest completely once the goal of an exercise has been achieved. If children need repetition to perfect a movement, a novel variation or a new goal is added each time.

In this classroom practical life exercises become increasingly automated, and integrated into larger projects, for example, preparing a meal for the class or planting a new garden. First, children plan the project, for example, by working on lists and diagrams, then collecting and purchasing whatever is needed. Next, they implement the project, for example, by preparing and cooking food, setting the table and serving, or digging, sowing and watering seeds. Finally, they clean up and put away the equipment ready for the next time it needs to be used.

Practical life exercises are further extended when school-age children go out of the classroom. In order to prepare for a field trip and participate effectively, children might need to know how to:

- make a telephone enquiry
- act on public transport
- wait in a queue
- pay for a ticket.

Practical life around the world

Practical life exercises reflect the culture of the children in the classroom. A hundred years of Montessori education across so many parts of the world has generated a fascinating array of practical life exercises. In early twentieth century European classrooms children used dressing frames with boot buttons and button hooks, and frames with the complicated lacing used on old-fashioned skates. Today, there are dressing frames with Velcro, and in classrooms near ski resorts, dressing frames with ski boot buckles. A list of suggested practical life exercises for Montessori schools in India includes teaching children how to grind spices, polish an earthen floor, make a flower garland and say namaste.

Practical life at home

Parents of children in Montessori schools are encouraged to give their children as many opportunities as possible to participate in family life in a meaningful way. They are encouraged to show their young children how everyday tasks are carried out in the family and to set up the home environment so children can carry out these tasks independently. These tasks might include, for example, pouring drinks, making fruit salad, folding laundry, raking leaves, setting the table and washing up. It then feels normal for children, as they grow older, to take on more responsibility, both for themselves and for others, for example, by preparing food for the family, vacuuming, or caring for family pets.

Parents and teachers of young children sometimes provide them with crockery and cutlery, stoves and sinks, and similar everyday equipment, in the form of toys. While pretending to do an activity with toy objects can be fun and fulfilling for little children in many ways, it demands little of them in terms of effort, precision and focus. Goal-directed activities with real objects, in contrast, require children to make an effort, to focus on the task and to use the objects precisely. In the Montessori view, these real-life activities provide a more substantial foundation for adapting to the social environment and for learning educational knowledge. They become the foundation on which the children's future freedom and independence are built.

Activity

Use the ideas in this chapter to prepare a practical life exercise for children you plan to work with. Match the exercise to the age and interests of the children. Present the exercise to individual children. Observe how the children incorporate the exercise into their freely chosen activity.

If possible, observe the same children using toy equipment and pretending they are taking part in everyday routines. How does the children's activity differ from their activity with real objects? How is it the same?

An alternative to rewards and punishments

Of all the Montessori exercises, those of practical life are probably the easiest to transport successfully from specialist Montessori classrooms into generalist early childhood settings.

Case study

A Montessori classroom had been established in a school in a disadvantaged area as part of a project to investigate whether an alternative approach might be more effective in assisting the children in the school to achieve educational success, despite the obstacles many of them faced. The other classrooms in the school were conventional ones.

One day, during playtime, two boys aged about seven, who were not part of the Montessori programme, were found taking large numbers of small stones from the garden and throwing them onto a pathway. The Montessori teacher observed as another teacher reprimanded the boys and told them to return the stones immediately. Resentful at being reprimanded, the boys began throwing the stones into the girls' toilets and, of course, found themselves in even more trouble.

The Montessori teacher asked if he could try a different approach. He showed the boys where to find an outdoor broom, a piece of chalk and a dustpan. Very carefully and precisely, concentrating on the task and not on the children, the teacher drew a chalk circle on the pathway. Slowly and deliberately, so the boys could see exactly the movements he used, he then swept some of the stones into the circle. He used the dustpan to pick up the stones and return them to the garden. He asked the boys if they would like to continue.

Much to the teachers' surprise, including the Montessori teacher, not only did the boys sweep up and return all the stones to the garden, but every day for the next week, the boys, of their own volition, continued to sweep paths until they had swept all the paths in the school. During this activity the boys displayed levels of effort and concentration they rarely if ever displayed in other school tasks.

Reflection point 〰

Why was the Montessori sweeping lesson a more effective intervention than reprimanding the children and demanding they return the stones to where they had found them? One possible reason is that reprimands and consequences imposed by adults force children to conform to standards that either have no meaning for them or are out of their reach. Similarly, if the boys had been offered a reward for cleaning up the stones, it is doubtful this would have made a difference. They had neither the equipment nor the know-how needed to solve the problem. In contrast, the Montessori sweeping lesson matched the boys' desire to do something active with the stones and to be in control. At the same time, it gave them an opportunity to do meaningful work that earned them respect. Above all, the lesson showed the boys, in a very practical and detailed way, exactly how to resolve the problem. The satisfaction of being able to do this for themselves was their reward. In this way, rather than having to respond to discipline imposed by others, the boys were able to discipline themselves, with the added bonus that they gained a skill they could transfer to all the other paths in the school.

Summary ▢

This chapter has introduced the Montessori exercises of practical life. These exercises fulfil children's interest in learning about the customs of their community and underpin the freedom children are given in Montessori classrooms. Through these exercises children learn how to manage everyday tasks and to contribute to the order and harmony of the environment. As they imitate and repeat sequences of precise movements, children refine both motor control and control of attention in preparation for the later demands of the school.

Things to think about

What do you think children gain from working with real objects at school and in the home?
What do you think children gain from pretending during their play to carry out everyday tasks using toy objects?

5

The exercises of the senses

Chapter objectives

- To introduce the second of the two foundation areas of the Montessori curriculum, the exercises of the senses.
- To consider the exercises of the senses both as a means for training the intellect in early childhood and a bridge to educational knowledge.
- To explore the relationship between abstraction and the imagination in early childhood.
- To introduce the three-period lesson.

The Montessori exercises of the senses are based on a principle that is best exemplified in the following way. When we see a car go by, the first thing we might notice is its red colour. Before long we might separate the idea of red from the other qualities of the car. Once the idea 'red' is no longer tied to the car, we can transfer it, for example, to an apple in the fruit bowl, a favourite shirt, or any one of an infinite number of red things. The idea 'red' has now become an abstract category we can use to classify any number of objects that share the same quality.

When we distance ourselves from concrete experience in order to extract or distil the essence of something attached to that reality, perhaps a quality, an idea or a concept, that essence becomes available to us as something we can think about in the abstract, even when the concrete experience is long gone. In other words, it becomes an intellectual resource, a resource for thinking. To abstract literally means to 'draw away'.

Through the exercises of the senses children construct in their minds an inventory of sensory impressions, a foundation, Montessori educators claim, for both the intellect and the imagination. Using precise hand movements, directed by the mind, children select and manipulate objects, this time to achieve intellectual goals based on sensory variation. The objects, known as the 'sensorial' materials, are the most distinctive of all Montessori objects. The pink tower, for example, is a Montessori icon.

What are the exercises of the senses and what is their purpose?

Sensory exploration is the signature of infancy. Tiny fingers seek out objects to grasp, lingering on irresistible textures, squeezing and prodding to find out more. Wide eyes gaze at faces, movement, colour and sparkle. Tantalizing objects find their way into little mouths. Little heads turn whether a captivating sound is familiar or not, and the special smell of mum or dad heightens the comfort of snuggling close.

Through the senses infants learn to recognize specific people and objects from a mass of otherwise indistinguishable impressions. For example, they might use sound, shape, size and smell to distinguish mother from father; shape, texture and size to distinguish a ball from a blanket; and taste, texture and smell to distinguish a banana from milk, however messy the consequences. In no time infants have co-opted adults to help them explore the sensory frontier. Pointing and grasping gestures clearly signal that an object should be fetched, and dropping objects from a height, or rolling them along the ground, are games that enchant the infant long after the adult helper has lost interest. With each advance in movement – rolling, sitting, crawling, walking – the frontier is pushed further outwards, and the store of sensory impressions expands with it.

In Montessori terms, the senses are the 'points of contact' through which young children absorb from the environment the impressions they use to construct the fabric of the mind and the intellect (Montessori, 1949/1982: 158). For this reason the Montessori approach places a great deal of emphasis on the education and exercising of the senses.

In Montessori Infant Communities, activities are often designed to isolate and bring to the child's conscious attention a specific sensory impression. For example, in a practical life exercise children might encounter a particularly fragrant flower or herb. The teacher will show the child how to smell and talk about the fragrance.

By the age of three children have collected enough sensory impressions to distinguish countless people and things. These impressions, however, are random and undifferentiated in the child's mind. In the Children's House, the exercises of the senses show children how to attend to specific sensory impressions, how to organize them, talk about them and retrieve them in an orderly way.

The Montessori exercises of the senses are based on sets of graded objects with design specifications as precise as those of scientific instruments. Each set of objects materializes, isolates and grades one quality. The qualities include texture, colour, volume, mass, length, taste, temperature, shape, sound and smell. These sets of graded objects help children to:

• bring sensory impressions to consciousness
• perceive finer and finer distinctions
• classify innumerable sensory impressions according to a limited set of abstract categories.

Exercises with these materials are matched to the following sensitive periods:

• From about the age of three children like to focus their attention on one sensory quality at a time, first perhaps texture, next maybe colour, later size.
• After the age of four children become interested in refining their perception. They focus their attention in order to be able to discriminate between increasingly fine variations, for example, between two slightly different shades of blue or two notes a semitone apart.

Activity

Observe a child engaged in freely chosen activity in each of the following age groups:

• under three
• between three and six.

Describe each child's sensory exploration, by recording:

• the sense, or senses, the child uses (touch, sight, hearing, taste, smell)
• objects that attract the child's attention and hold their interest, and the qualities of the objects (e.g. texture, colour, shape, size)
• how the child moves and manipulates objects
• any communication (gestures and language).

How is the sensory exploration of the children the same? How is it different?

Abstracting sensory qualities in concrete form, according to Montessori educators, enables young children to refine and order their perceptions and, on this foundation, build a framework for the intellect. These 'materialised abstractions' (Montessori, 1949/1982: 162) are also understood, in the Montessori tradition, as raw material for the imagination.

Abstraction and imagination

Abstraction is the process of extracting from concrete reality an essence, or an idea, that then can become a resource for thinking. Imagination is the ability to think of things not immediately present to the senses. Abstraction and imagination are considered in the Montessori tradition to be interdependent. Once children have assembled in their mind an orderly catalogue of perceptions, varying on the basis of finer and finer distinctions experienced in the real world, the imagination can select from and re-assemble these perceptions to create an unlimited number of images, possibilities, and impossibilities. A child's catalogue of sensory qualities, abstracted from reality, is the source of the child's imaginative and creative potential. Reality is thus the starting point for the imagination in early childhood (Montessori, 1949/1982: 161).

Educational knowledge

School introduces children to educational knowledge organized, on the basis of abstract categories, into various subjects, or disciplines, such as mathematics, history, astronomy and biology. In the Montessori tradition the exercises of the senses offer young children, through playful activities with concrete objects, 'keys' they can later use to enter these domains of knowledge with ease and enjoyment.

The design of the Montessori sensorial materials

In the sensorial materials are concentrated the most distinctive features of all the Montessori materials.

A direct purpose and an indirect purpose

Each exercise of the senses has a direct purpose and an indirect purpose. The direct purpose of each set of objects is understood by the child, for example:

• matching the bells according to pitch
• building the pink tower with exactness and control.

The indirect purpose foreshadows a future developmental step, for example:

• refining auditory discrimination to prepare for future study in music
• refining discrimination of volume to prepare for future study in mathematics.

An aesthetically pleasing appearance

The objects are aesthetically pleasing, in sound, texture, colour and shape, enticing children to use them. They are always kept clean and in perfect condition.

The isolation of a single quality

Each set of graded objects isolates a single quality. The isolation of one quality attracts attention and limits 'the field of the child's consciousness to the object of the lesson' (Montessori, 1912/1964: 224). For example, the pink tower isolates the quality of volume. The tower is made of 10 cubes, the sides of each cube varying in length, one centimetre at a time, from the smallest (1 cm^3) to the largest (10 cm^3). The cubes do not vary in colour (pink), texture (glossy painted surface) or material (wood). Because a sensory quality is isolated in each set of objects, children can compare the objects on the basis of variations in this one quality without being distracted by other variables.

A control of error

A control of error enables children to do an exercise successfully yet independently. It allows children to self-correct as they go, guiding their judgement and encouraging precision. For example, for the pink tower to be both stable and neat, the cubes must be placed in order, from the largest at the bottom to the smallest at the top. A control of error may be mechanical, perceptual, or both. A mechanical control of error might be an inset not fitting into a frame or a tower falling over. A perceptual control of error might be an array or sequence that does not look, sound or feel right.

A limited quantity of objects in each set

The quantity of objects in each set is limited. The number of bells, for example, is limited to the number of notes in an octave, and the number of colour tablets is limited to the number of primary, secondary and terti-

ary colours. The number of objects in many sets is limited to 10, in preparation for future study in mathematics.

A limited number of sets

Only one of each set is placed in the environment. This makes the material
special, and encourages children to use it with care and respect.

A limited use

Each set of objects has an exact use to limit confusion and distraction, and to
promote interest and concentration. Some objects are small, others have a
small knob requiring careful use of the pincer grip. Each piece of material Dr
Montessori (1948/1967: 102–5) describes as a 'straight and limited road which
leads to a goal and keeps the learner from wandering aimlessly about'.

Language

Each set of sensorial objects is designed to isolate one quality so children
can compare variations in that quality. When children use a set of objects
in an exact and purposeful way, their perception is trained so they are able
to discriminate between increasingly fine variations of that quality. The
design of the objects means, moreover, that children experience each quality as if it were an abstract category, even if, for now, the category is materialized in concrete form.

The sensorial objects, being concrete, are not transferable, however, to times
and places beyond the classroom. If the categories materialized in the sensorial objects are to become raw material for the intellect and the imagination,
they need to be portable. This is achieved by giving children language to label
each quality, and its variations. Language is said, in the Montessori tradition,
to 'fix' the perception of a quality in the child's memory.

The three-period lesson

Children are given language for the variable qualities of the sensorial materials in a 'three-period' lesson. This lesson is not only used with the sense
exercises, but in all areas of the Montessori curriculum. Each lesson teaches
two or three related words, echoing contrasts in the material. Learning
words related, for example, through contrast, makes them easier to remember than words in isolation (Montessori, 1912/1964: 178). As its name
suggests, the lesson has three parts, or periods (Table 5.1).

The lesson is delivered with a light touch and the most economical use of language possible; there is no irrelevant chatter or conversation. If in the second or third period, the child makes an error, at a later time, and without correcting the child, the teacher returns to the first period. Montessori educators see no value in correction. If children know something, they will show you or tell you. If they don't know, they need a lesson. If, through correction, a child becomes conscious of making an error, everything else is pushed out of the child's mind, making it more difficult for the child to learn.

Table 5.1   The three-period lesson

	Teaching steps	*Language examples*
First period	The teacher indicates a quality materialized in an object and gives the child a word for this quality. The child begins to associate the language (what we say) with the perception (what we see and touch).	*This is red.* *This is blue.* *This is yellow.* *This is rough.* *This is smooth.* *This is a triangle.* *This is a square.* *This is a circle.*
Second period	The teacher names a quality materialized in an object and the child moves to identify the object. The teacher elicits a variety of movements from the child. In this the most extended and varied part of the lesson, the child and the teacher collaborate, the child recognizing the object with the quality that corresponds to the language provided by the teacher.	*Give me the red.* *Which one is rough?* *Show me the triangle* *Where is the red one?* *Can you find the rough one?* *Put the triangle back in its frame.*
Third period	The teacher slips into the third period, without the child noticing, by casually asking questions. The responsibility for identifying the quality, using both movement and language, is handed over to the child, and the teacher is able to verify the child has learned the names.	*What's this again?* *Do you remember what this is?* *Can you tell me what this is?*

Reflection point 〰

In many early childhood settings a lesson begins with the teacher eliciting what children already know. To begin a lesson about shapes, for example, a teacher might hold up for the whole class to see a square cut-out of paper, a picture of a square or a square-shaped object and ask: 'What's this?' Because there has been no prior teaching, some children will attend to the object (a piece of paper, a picture, a toy) rather than the shape. Some will know the correct term for the shape (square), some will not. While many children are still learning to attend to the shape rather than the object, the teacher will add a further complication by asking about the properties of the shape, for example: 'How many sides does it have?' These lessons often involve a lot of conversation in which children contribute their guesses as well as personal experiences, sometimes related to the topic and sometimes not.

From a Montessori perspective this type of lesson begins with the third period. Children without prior knowledge can only guess the answer and it soon becomes apparent if they are wrong. The surrounding chat serves to confuse rather than clarify.

In the equivalent Montessori lesson, children trace around three wooden insets varying only in shape (triangle, square, circle), before placing the insets in matching frames. Then, in a three-period lesson, children are given the names of the shapes. There is no guessing, and no unrelated chatter. Only then do children look for those shapes embodied in objects in the environment. At a later time, with different material, children will learn about the properties of the shapes, such as the number of sides.

The stages of a sensorial lesson

The three-stage pattern used in practical life lessons reappears in lessons showing children how to do the exercises of the senses, with the addition of a three-period lesson in the presentation stage. The three stages are:

- the teacher's presentation (including a three-period language lesson)
- the child's independent work
- the child's use of the knowledge in another context.

A sample lesson: the colour tablets

When children enter the Children's House, they often recognize and know the names of many colours. The colour tablets organize this knowledge in a systematic way. The tablets vary in colour, but not in shape or size. In early Children's Houses they were made by winding embroidery silk round small rectangular wooden tablets, leaving an edge at each end for holding the tablet without touching the silk. The shimmering silk threads have mostly been replaced in today's schools with glossy enamel paint. The beauty of these tablets, and the care required to pick them up without touching the colour, is a motive for concentrated and careful use.

The colour tablets are stored in three boxes. Box 1 is presented to children of about three when they display an interest in colour. This box contains six tablets, one pair of each of the primary colours: red, blue and yellow (Table 5.2).

Table 5.2 Presenting Colour Box 1

Opening phase	The teacher begins by: • taking Box 1 from the shelf and bringing it to the table • opening the box and placing the lid underneath.
Matching	Using rehearsed movements, slowly and with precision, the teacher: • removes the tablets one by one, places them on the table and mixes them • selects a tablet • asks the child to find one 'just like it' • demonstrates how to match the tablets as a pair. The child matches the other two pairs. Finally, the six tablets are arranged in an array of three matching pairs. The child mixes the tablets and repeats the matching as many times as desired.
Three-period lesson	1. The teacher points to each tablet in turn and names the colour: *This is red.* *This is blue.* *This is yellow.* 2. The teacher mixes up the tablets and asks the child to indicate colours with questions such as the following: *Give me the red.* *Which one is blue?* *Can you show me the yellow one?* *Where is the red?* *Put the blue one back in the box.* *Find the red one.* *Would you like to find the yellow one?* 3. When sure the child will be successful, the teacher asks: *What's this?* *Do you remember what this is?* *Can you tell me what this is?*
Closing phase	When the child is ready to finish the work, the teacher closes the presentation by: • showing how to put the colour tablets back in the box, and closing the lid • putting the objects away.

Independent work

After the lesson the child can choose the work at any time. Observing the child's independent work with Box 1 indicates to the teacher when to offer the child Box 2. The child's own work is the most important part of the exercise. If a sense exercise is well matched to a child's sensitive period, the child will often repeat the exercise over and over again. This prolonged activity not only develops acuity of perception but also concentration and fine motor control.

The teacher observes the child's independent work carefully. If at this stage children are rough with the materials, or are unable to use them with precision, they are often redirected to a vigorous practical life exercise. If they use the materials for free play, for example, stacking the colour tablets, they are offered more appropriate materials such as plain blocks. If they want to use a different sense, for example, touching the tablets instead of looking at them, they might be given a lesson with materials designed to exercise the sense of touch.

Using the knowledge in another context

There are many ways children transfer knowledge of colours to other contexts. They might match the tablets to objects in the room, or to items of clothing. The knowledge is also applied and extended in the creative arts. The teacher incorporates into the environment as many opportunities as possible for children to make this transition.

Extension exercises

Matching

Colour Box 2 is used for extended matching. This box contains eleven pairs of tablets, the three pairs of primary colours again, three pairs of secondary colours (orange, green, purple), three pairs of tertiary colours (pink, grey, brown), and a pair of black and a pair of white tablets. The teacher presents this box in the same way as Box 1, giving three-period lessons as needed to teach the names of the colours.

Grading

Colour Box 3 is used for grading. In this box, for each colour (primary, secondary and tertiary), there is a set of seven tablets, each a different shade, from lightest to darkest. Black and white reappear in this box as the darkest and lightest shades of grey. The box contains 63 tablets in all.

To show a child how to grade the tablets, the teacher takes from the box seven shades of one colour, perhaps the child's favourite, isolates the darkest, the middle shade and the lightest, and puts the four interim shades to one side. The teacher shows the child how to put the darkest shade to the left, the middle shade next to it, and finally the lightest shade to complete the array, before mixing them up. The teacher takes the darkest shade and asks the child for the tablet that is 'just a little bit different', continuing until all three shades are graded again. When the child is ready, the teacher shows how to grade all seven shades.

When the teacher is sure the child has grasped the concept of grading, more exact language is introduced (light, dark; lighter, darker; lightest, darkest), again using the three-period lesson. As the child's independent work progresses, the level of difficulty is gradually increased. The child might, for example, mix all the shades of two colours, 14 tablets in all, and grade those. Eventually, the child mixes up, sorts and grades all 63 tablets in the box to create a very beautiful array.

Memory games

In all the sense exercises, just before the child's interest wanes, and if the child has not discovered it for themselves by observing other children, the teacher introduces the next level of difficulty and a more refined level of discrimination. As the finest levels of discrimination are reached, the teacher introduces the memory games. In these games the child holds the 'image' of the sensory quality in their mind. For example, in the memory game with the Montessori bells the child carries the set of brown bells to the other side of the room. The child returns to the white bells, strikes one, then walks across the room with the pitch in mind and strikes the brown bells, one at a time, to find the one that matches.

When playing memory games with the colour tablets, the child takes one tablet of each pair to a mat or table on the other side of the room. The child then chooses one colour, looks at it and puts it down. Holding the colour as a mental image only, the child crosses the room to fetch the matching tablet. Similar memory games involve grading.

Training the intellect

While matching, grading and memorizing, the child's attention is directed progressively from 'a few stimuli strongly contrasting, to many stimuli in gradual differentiation always more fine and imperceptible' (Montessori, 1912/1964: 184). As children actively compare objects, looking for contrasts and similarities, they develop what Dr Montessori described as the 'great intellectual activities' of attention and judgement. This training occurs as children attend first to one object, then to another, and back to the first object, over and over again. Dr Montessori (1918/1965b: 60) described this special kind of intellectualized discrimination and judgement as the 'polarisation of the attention'.

In adult life, the ability to 'polarise the attention' between several comparable elements for extended periods of time lies at the heart of problem-solving and the making of informed judgements. A trivial example is a jigsaw puzzle in which we compare the colours and shapes on the pieces with a picture, and we compare the shapes of the pieces with the missing parts of the puzzle. The Montessori sense exercises can be thought of as a series of puzzles in which children are making judgements, one quality at a time, requiring progressively finer and finer discrimination.

Through the exercises of the senses children become conscious of the abstract means used by the people around them to attend to, order and classify otherwise random sensory impressions, including impressions of texture, colour, volume, mass, length, taste, temperature, sound and shape. The variations children learn to perceive using the materials and the language they are given to talk about these variations become the foundation for later work in the creative arts and the educational disciplines.

Case study

Luca, who is just three, has started at a Children's House where the children and teachers speak English. Luca has just arrived with his family from abroad and speaks no English. From the first day he is shown how to do exercises of practical life and exercises of the senses. He begins work immediately. In six months he is working in all areas of the classroom, including with many language games and activities. He chatters with his friends and expresses his needs in English.

Reflection point

The concrete objects, explicit presentations and individual and small group lessons in a Montessori setting enable children who do not speak the language of the classroom to begin work with the curriculum materials from the moment they arrive, learning the language as they work. They do not have to put their learning on hold until after they have mastered the language. Similarly, children

(Continued)

(Continued)
with diverse learning needs and gifts can engage with the curriculum while working at their own pace and following their own interests.

The Montessori sensorial materials are sometimes acknowledged as the forerunners of the puzzles and concrete problem-solving tasks now commonly found in all early childhood settings (MacNaughton and Williams, 2004: 364).

Types of sense exercises

There are between 20 and 30 sets of Montessori sensorial materials and, for each set, there is a progression of exercises. The exercises train the following senses:

- visual
- tactile
- taste and smell
- baric and thermic
- stereognostic
- auditory.

The visual sense

The colour tablets belong to the group of materials that train the visual sense. Other materials in this group train children to perceive finer and finer differences in, for example, thickness, volume, length and shape. Many of these materials prepare children for the study of mathematics.

- There are 10 objects in many sets.
- The dimensions of the objects, and their variations, are metric units.

When children first enter the Children's House, they are introduced to the solid cylinders. Knobless cylinders are a later extension of this exercise (Table 5.3).

In other early exercises children build a pink tower, a broad stair and a stair with the long rods (Table 5.4). They are shown how to do the basic exercises but many possible variations and combinations are not presented, leaving the children to discover these for themselves.

Table 5.3 Cylinders

Solid cylinders	
Description	Four wooden blocks, each with a row of ten cylindrical holes and ten knobbed wooden cylinders that fit exactly into the holes (40 cylinders in total).
	Block 1: cylinders vary in one dimension (height).
	Block 2: cylinders vary in two dimensions (diameter, circumference).
	Blocks 3 and 4: cylinders vary in three dimensions (height, diameter, circumference).
Age	From 3 years.
Exercise	1. Take the cylinders out of the holes.
	2. Mix the cylinders and replace them into the holes.
	3. Repeat as often as the child wants.
Progression of work	1. Work with one block at a time.
	2. Use two or more blocks together, mixing all the cylinders together before replacing them.
	3. Work with all four blocks (40 cylinders).
Language	Short-tall, thick-thin.
Knobless cylinders	
Description	Four boxes of cylinders identical to the solid cylinders, but without the blocks and knobs, each set a different colour (blue, red, green, yellow).
Age	3–5 years.
Exercises	1. Grade cylinders.
	2. Compare one graded series of cylinders with another.
	3. Build towers.
	4. Experiment.

Indirectly preparing for geometry

There are two series of exercises for the visual sense that foreshadow the study of geometry: the geometry cabinet and the constructive triangles.

The geometry cabinet has six drawers, containing yellow wooden frames and matching blue insets in different shapes, each with a tiny blue knob. Children, from the age of three, match insets to frames and learn the names of the shapes, beginning with the strongest contrasts (triangle, square, circle). Before matching the insets to the frames, children trace with their fingers around both the frame and the inset. This helps them remember the shapes and match inset to frame more exactly. It also indirectly prepares for handwriting. Over time children work with over 30 shapes, including different sizes of circles, and different types of triangles, quadrilaterals and polygons. Once children know the names of shapes, they recognize them in the environment, and use them, for example, in artwork.

The geometry cabinet is accompanied by three series of cards. The shapes on the cards match exactly the shapes in the cabinet. The shapes on the first series are filled in, on the second series they are outlined with a thick line and on the third series with a thin line. In other words, the shapes become increasingly abstract. Children match the cards to the insets, and use them in grading and memory games. The geometry cabinet exercises draw children into the study of geometry.

Table 5.4 Pink Tower, Broad Stair and Long Rods

Pink Tower	
Description	A series of 10 pink cubes, varying in volume from 1 cm³ to 10 cm³.
Age	3 years.
Exercises	1. Mix the cubes on a mat.
	2. Build the tower.
	3. Play memory games.
Language	Big-small.
Broad Stair	
Description	A series of 10 brown, wooden square prisms, 20 cm long, varying in thickness from the thinnest (1 cm²) to the thickest (10 cm²).
Age	From 3 years.
Exercises	1. Mix the prisms on a mat.
	2. Build the stair.
	3. Play memory games.
Language	Thick-thin.
Long Rods	
Description	A series of 10 red, wooden rods, varying in length from 10 cm to 1 metre.
Age	From 3 years.
Exercises	1. Mix the rods on a mat.
	2. Build the stair.
	3. Play memory games.
Language	Long-short.

Case study 🗁

Four-year-old Finn is working with the drawer of polygons. The insets are spread on the mat ready for matching to frames. Finn picks up the decagon by its knob, twirls it rapidly and says, 'Look, a circle!'

Children progress from the geometry cabinet to the constructive triangles. These are boxes of wooden triangles used to construct many of the shapes introduced with the geometry cabinet. The constructive triangles are perhaps the most sophisticated of all the sensorial materials. Beyond the age of nine children are still using them to study geometry.

Indirectly preparing for botany

The botany cabinet echoes the geometry cabinet in design and use. It has three drawers and the insets, coloured green, are leaf shapes. The children trace around the shapes with a special wooden stylus. They learn scientific names for the shapes, and look for them in the leaves of plants in the indoor and outdoor environment. Children work with the botany cabinet between the ages of three and four. It becomes the basis of botany study in the six to nine classroom.

Case study

A teacher uses three-period lessons to teach one or two children the names of leaf shapes in the botany cabinet. Suddenly the classroom is inundated with leaves! The children focus on leaves in the park, in the playground, in the garden at home. They bring leaves into the classroom to match them with shapes in the botany cabinet. A passion for the study of leaves sweeps through the whole class. A parent tells of going for walks with her daughter, who delightedly collects leaves saying: 'This is linear; that's sagittate ...'

Indirectly preparing for algebra

The binomial and trinomial cubes are three-dimensional wooden puzzles contained in cube-shaped wooden boxes. The binomial cube materializes the algebraic binomial $(a + b)^3$ where $a > b$. It is constructed in two layers of coloured blocks (the a layer and the b layer; a total of two cubes and six prisms). Each block materializes one term in the expansion of the binomial. The square faces of the blocks are coloured (a^2 = red; b^2 = blue). The rectangular faces (a x b) are black. The children use a two-dimensional representation of the binomial pattern as a base. They build the two layers of the cube onto the base, matching the faces by size and colour.

The trinomial cube is an expansion of the binomial cube, materializing the algebraic trinomial $(a + b + c)^3$ where $a > b > c$. The trinomial is constructed using three layers of blocks (three cubes and 24 prisms in total). Yellow is used for the c^2 faces. Children from the age of three love these puzzles, even though it will not be until they are 11 or 12 that they work with the algebra used by Dr Montessori to design the puzzle.

Activity

Because the specifications are so exact, Montessori materials that train the visual sense can only be purchased from specialist manufacturers. In many early childhood settings, however, you will find puzzles with similar features, or puzzles that can be adapted using Montessori principles.
   Observe children using such puzzles and record your observations.

Many sensorial materials for training senses other than sight are much easier for teachers to make for themselves. Here are some examples.

The sense of touch

Before children exercise the sense of touch, they are shown how to sensitize the tips of their fingers by dipping them in warm water and drying them on a hand towel. They then trace over the different textures with the lightest of touches, using the two fingers of their dominant hand. This action prepares for handwriting (Table 5.5).

Fabric boxes (Table 5.6) are a favourite touch exercise that prepares children for work in art and craft. Beautiful fabrics are chosen that contrast not only in texture, but also in colour and weight. The fabrics are stored in gorgeous boxes that children find irresistible.

The senses of taste and smell

Tasting and smelling bottles train children to discriminate between different tastes and smells in the environment, preparing for the study of nutrition (Table 5.7).

The baric sense and the thermic sense

The baric tablets prepare children for measuring mass, while the thermic tablets and bottles prepare for measuring temperature (Table 5.8).

Table 5.5 Touch boards; touch tablets

Touch boards	
Description	Two small boards made out of polished wood.
	Touch Board 1: half the board is covered with the finest grade of sandpaper.
	Touch Board 2: five parallel strips of finest sandpaper glued onto the board creating alternating rough and smooth strips.
Age	3 years.
Exercises	Touch the sand paper and say 'rough'. Touch the wood and say 'smooth'.
	Use a blindfold to increase the challenge.
Language	Rough-smooth.
Touch tablets	
Description	Five pairs of identical, small rectangular tablets covered in sandpaper, the roughness and colour of each pair varying slightly, the colour becoming darker as the sandpaper becomes rougher.
Age	3 years.
Exercises	1. Mix the tablets.
	2. Match the pairs.
	3. Grade the tablets.
	4. Play memory games.
	Use a blindfold to increase the challenge.
Language	Rougher-smoother.

Table 5.6 Fabric boxes

Description	Box 1: five pairs of fabric swatches, each a different texture both rough and smooth, cut the same size with pinking shears.
	Box 2: five pairs of different rough-textured swatches.
	Box 3: five pairs of different smooth-textured swatches.
Age	3 years.
Exercises	1. Mix the swatches.
	2. Touch the swatches lightly to find ones that 'feel the same'.
	3. Grade the swatches.
	4. Play memory games.
	Use a blindfold to increase the challenge.
Language	Rough-rougher, smooth-smoother.

Table 5.7   Tasting and smelling bottles

Tasting bottles	
Description	Four pairs of identical bottles with eye-droppers.
	Each pair of bottles contains a solution with a different taste (sweet, salty, acidic, bitter). Colour code as an extra guide.
	Caution: Containers must not resemble medicine bottles. Monitor carefully for hygiene.
Age	4 years.
Exercises	1. Match the tastes by using the dropper to place a drop of solution on the tongue (without letting the dropper touch the tongue).
	2. Use the four taste categories to identify tastes in food at mealtimes.
	Hold the nose to increase the challenge.
Language	Sweet, salty, acidic, bitter.
Smelling bottles	
Description	Three pairs of identical spice bottles.
	Each pair of bottles contains a cotton ball infused with the same odour (e.g. perfume, a spice or herb such as cinnamon or basil, an aromatic oil such as eucalyptus).
	Colour code as an extra guide.
Age	3–4 years.
Exercises	1. Match the odours by opening the lid of each bottle and wafting the odour towards the nose.
	2. Compare the odours to odours in the indoor and outdoor environments (e.g. cooking, flowers, fruit, pets).

Table 5.8   Baric tablets; thermic tablets and bottles

Baric tablets	
Description	Five pairs of tablets, identical in size, stored in a box.
	Each pair varies incrementally in weight and colour (from heavy/dark to light).
Age	4 years.
Exercises	1. Match pairs by hefting, i.e. holding them away from the body in upturned hands.
	2. Grade the tablets.
	3. Play memory games.
	Use a blindfold to increase the challenge.
Language	Heavy-light, heavier-lighter.
Thermic tablets	
Description	Four pairs of tablets, identical in size, stored in a box, each pair made of different material (felt, wood, stone, metal).
Age	3–4 years.

Table 5.8

Exercises	1. Match pairs by placing hands on top of each tablet.
	2. Grade the tablets.
	3. Play memory games.
	4. Compare with different materials in the environment.
	Use a blindfold to increase the challenge (or try it with bare feet!)
Language	Felt, wood, stone, metal.

Thermic bottles	
Description	Four pairs of identical metal bottles in a wooden container.
	Colour code as an extra guide.
Age	From 3½ years.
Exercises	1. The adult fills each pair of bottles with water of the same temperature (iced, body temperature, tepid, safely hot). One from each pair is lined up as control. Mix the remainder.
	The child holds a control bottle in the left hand and with the right hand searches for one that feels the same.
	2. Grade the bottles.
Language	Hot-cold, hotter-colder.

The stereognostic sense

The term 'stereognostic' was coined by Dr Montessori to describe the way we use our senses to differentiate between three-dimensional shapes. Sorting games and mystery bags train this ability (Table 5.9).

Table 5.9   Sorting game and mystery bag

Sorting game	
Description	A large dish and four smaller dishes stored on a felt-lined tray.
	The large dish contains a collection of up to 20 small objects of four types (mixtures of different objects or four types of the same object, e.g. shells, beads, pasta, buttons).
	Change regularly to maintain interest.
Age	From 3 years.
Exercises	1. Choose an object, look and feel, then find one just like it. Sort all objects into the small dishes.
	2. Grade objects according to size and shape.

Mystery bag	
Description	A beautiful drawstring bag containing a selection of objects, both familiar (e.g. ball, bell, brush) and unfamiliar. Change the objects regularly to maintain the surprise.
Age	From 3½ years.
Exercises	1. Put your hand into the bag and choose an object. Name the object before pulling it out.
	2. Play the game in a group.

Geometry solids

Work with the geometry solids (Table 5.10) leads into the study of solid geometry.

Table 5.10   Geometry solids

Description	A set of three-dimensional blue wooden shapes (sphere, cube, cylinder, cone, square prism, triangular prism, square pyramid, triangular pyramid, ellipsoid, ovoid) in a basket.
	A set of wooden bases, outlined in blue, to match the faces of the solids (circle, square, triangle, rectangle).
Age	From 3½ years.
Exercises	1. The teacher chooses three contrasting solids, one at a time, feeling each one carefully all over with both hands. The solid is then given to the child to feel with both hands, before it is placed on the mat.
	2. The child learns the names of the solids in a three-period lesson.
	Over time, the child learns all the solids.
Extension	The child matches the solids to the bases, experimenting to discover that some solids have two bases (e.g. prisms), some one (e.g. cone) and some none (i.e. the sphere, ellipsoid and ovoid sit on a point only).

The auditory sense

Exercises to train the auditory sense include sound boxes, listening games and the Montessori bells. Sound boxes train children to perceive differences in sound quality (Table 5.11).

Listening games

The ability to listen underpins children's success at school. Difficulty with listening is the origin of many learning problems. Some children, however, do not learn this skill on their own.

In the Montessori Children's House and classrooms for six- to nine-year-olds, children learn how to listen, especially in a group, during grace and courtesy lessons. Listening games teach accurate listening, and how to compare and make judgements about sounds. Montessori teachers have a large repertoire of these games with endless variations, for individuals and groups (Table 5.12).

Table 5.11 Sound boxes

Description	Two wooden boxes, one with a red lid and one with a blue lid.
	Inside each box are six cylinders with tops colour-coded to match the lid of their box.
	In each cylinder are different amounts and sizes of beans so that each cylinder, when shaken, makes a slightly different sound graded from loudest to softest.
	For each cylinder in the red box, there is a cylinder in the blue box that makes an identical sound.
Age	From 3½ years.
Exercises	1. Line up the red cylinders as a control and mix up the blue cylinders.
	Shake a red cylinder, first beside one ear, then, changing hands, beside the other ear.
	Search among the blue cylinders for the matching sound, shaking each in the same way.
	Match all the pairs.
	2. Grade the cylinders from loud to soft.
Language	Loud-soft, louder-softer.

Table 5.12 Listening games

Mystery sound	Prepare a tray of objects (e.g. a jug of water, a glass, some paper, a jar of beads, a small broom, a comb, a book).
	Ask a child to turn around and look away.
	1. The teacher, or another child, performs an action (e.g. pours water, crumples paper, shakes the jar, turns pages).
	2. The child identifies the sound.
Statue games	Children move around a space, then freeze on a signal (e.g. a bell).
	Variations to increase the challenge include freezing on one leg, as an animal or a character.
Blindfold games	A blindfolded child points in the direction of a bell softly rung by a teacher or child, stationary or moving.
	Increase the challenge with a ticking clock, or ask the blindfolded child to identify, for example, dropped objects, animal voices or voices of classmates.
	A blindfolded child can be taken for a walk to listen for different sounds.

The Montessori bells prepare for the study of music. Exercises with the bells train children to perceive differences in pitch, and to learn the names of the notes. These exercises play a pivotal role in a pathway prepared for children to lead them from sensory exploration to the study of music.

A prepared path to culture

On our visit to the Montessori Children's House in Chapter 2 we heard, drifting over the hum of the classroom, the sound of musical bells. A child was striking a series of small, shiny, mushroom-shaped bells, playing up and down the major scale and matching bells of the same pitch. The notes echo around the classroom, as much a part of the sensory background of the classroom as colour and texture. This exercise is one in a progressive series of exercises that originates in the earliest sensory exploration of sound in infancy and extends, step by step, towards the study of music as a domain of educational knowledge. This progression is known in the Montessori tradition as a prepared path to culture, in this case, to musical culture.

Sensory exploration in infancy

The pathway to musical culture begins with the infinite variety of sounds first heard by a baby. From this amorphous mass of sound the child gradually distinguishes, for example, the sound of the mother's voice, the sounds of human language and of animals, the sounds of nature and of machines, loud and soft sounds, and, of course, musical sounds. At home, and in a Montessori Infant Community, children hear different types of music, sing songs and play simple instruments.

Discovering sensory 'keys' in the Children's House

In the Children's House children encounter three sensory 'keys' in preparation for the study of music:

1. Pitch (singing; bells).
2. Sound quality (percussion instruments; sound boxes).
3. Rhythm (rhythmic movement on the line; clapping rhythm patterns).

Case study

Ava, who is playing the bells when we visit the Children's House, is learning to distinguish variation in pitch. In an echo of the exercises of practical life, she has been shown how to:

- use a striker to obtain the clearest note possible from each bell
- stop each note resonating before striking and listening to the next one.

In this way each note is isolated, ensuring she gains a clear impression of its pitch.

On the day of our visit Ava chooses a matching exercise. There are two series of eight bells, one on white stands and one on brown stands. The white series is the control, lined up on wooden bases painted to represent an octave of the piano keyboard, one white bell for each 'white' note of the major scale.

Ava begins the exercise by playing up the major scale on the white bells, from middle C to its octave, and then down again, before mixing up the brown bells. She strikes the first white bell to hear middle C and a brown bell to listen for the same pitch. She strikes middle C again, and another brown bell, searching for middle C among the brown bells to pair with the white one. In the same way she pairs all the bells, checking her work at the end by playing up and down the scale, first on the white bells and then on the brown bells, the white bells acting as a control of error.

Later Ava sings the notes, learns their names and plays grading and memory games with them. She will learn how to write music using movable wooden notes and clefs on a staff painted on a wooden board before eventually writing notes directly onto manuscript paper. Over time she will create her own compositions, and transfer her knowledge and skill to singing, playing musical instruments and reading music.

Planting 'seeds' of knowledge in the early school years

The incremental progression of musical exercises extends into the classroom for six- to nine-year-olds, where children are offered the 'seeds' of musical knowledge. To refine further their training in pitch and to extend their knowledge of musical notation, theory, composition and performance, the children work with 25 movable tone bars on a wooden keyboard spanning two octaves.

The progress made by children along the pathway to musical culture is driven by interest, imagination and creativity. Along the way, in the prepared environment, children encounter materials for learning about musical instruments, composers and musical styles from different times and places. They also have opportunities to attend musical performances, to sing and play musical instruments and to stage performances of their own.

A prepared path to culture as teaching repertoire

The Montessori prepared path to musical culture is a teaching repertoire spanning three stages (Table 5.13).

Table 5.13   Prepared path to musical culture

Sensory exploration (0–3)	Infants recognize music as something distinct from other types of sensory experience.
Sensory keys (3–6)	Children encounter sensory 'keys' they will later use to enter the domain of musical knowledge.
Seeds of knowledge (6–9)	Children are given 'seeds' of musical knowledge as starting points for studying the field of music. They are shown connections between music and other fields of knowledge, e.g. sound experiments in science.

A similar path from sensory exploration to educational knowledge can be traced for each subject area of the Montessori curriculum, including language, mathematics, history, geography, science and art. These paths have many parallels and interconnections. For example, the way children learn to write and read music parallels the way they learn to write and read language.

With such an expansive and interconnected repertoire at their fingertips, Montessori teachers always have an activity just right for each child, whatever the child's stage of development, interests or needs. In any Montessori classroom at any time there is much individual variation in both the sequence and pace of learning. While the teacher's repertoire is prolific, the scope of an individual child's work at any one time is comparatively limited, no one child covering all possible exercises. From each child's perspective, there are always new and interesting activities and games, each one with the potential for a new discovery.

Because children are free to move around the classroom, they can listen to lessons and watch activities they have not yet tried, at their own level and beyond, and they can review earlier ones. If the Children's House is located near the classroom for six- to nine-year-olds, small children can take 'an intellectual walk' (Montessori, 1918/1965b: 5) to see older children using familiar materials for more advanced work and older children can return with greater understanding to the sensorial materials in the Children's House. When small children see older children reviewing these materials, their interest in them is rekindled.

The Montessori curriculum is not implemented in a way that forces children to learn vast amounts of academic content. Instead, the incremental steps along the prepared paths to culture are another manifestation of the order that Dr Montessori discovered captures and holds children's interest, and helps them concentrate. The exercises of the senses are matched to the young child's interest in ordering sensory impressions and in exact movement. Similarly, when older children are given both an impression of how a field of knowledge is ordered as a whole, and exact starting points for exploring that field in an orderly way, they are able to satisfy their intense interest in knowing and understanding the world around them.

Summary

This chapter has introduced the Montessori exercises of the senses. These exercises match the young child's love of sensory exploration. They also train intellectual skills of comparison and judgement and help children build an inventory of impressions they can use in later intellectual and imaginative endeavours.

Things to think about

The transition from one stage of schooling to the next can be difficult for some children, putting the quality of their education at risk. Critical transitions in early childhood include:

• home or day care to pre-school
• pre-school to school.

1. What does the Montessori approach offer educators concerned with enhancing the critical educational transitions of early childhood?
2. From your own repertoire of early childhood activities can you map a pathway from infancy to the first years of school in one field of knowledge (e.g. mathematics, history, geography, science)?
3. What do you think are the advantages, and disadvantages, of a teaching repertoire as incremental, interconnected and extensive as the Montessori one?

Montessori language

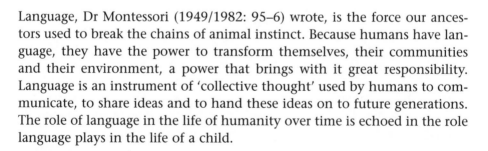

Chapter objectives

- To outline the interwoven development of movement and language in early childhood.
- To explore how language education in Montessori early childhood settings builds on the foundation exercises of practical life and the senses.
- To highlight the distinctive design features of the Montessori language materials.
- To describe some Montessori spoken language activities.
- To review the Montessori pathway to writing and reading.

Language, Dr Montessori (1949/1982: 95–6) wrote, is the force our ancestors used to break the chains of animal instinct. Because humans have language, they have the power to transform themselves, their communities and their environment, a power that brings with it great responsibility. Language is an instrument of 'collective thought' used by humans to communicate, to share ideas and to hand these ideas on to future generations. The role of language in the life of humanity over time is echoed in the role language plays in the life of a child.

In the lessons of grace and courtesy children in Montessori early childhood settings learn language for interacting with others at home, at school and in the wider community. The language that accompanies the Montessori exercises of the senses helps children organize and hold sensory perceptions in the mind as a resource for thinking and imagining. The Montessori language curriculum builds on these starting points.

Language and movement

Children's language development, in the Montessori view, is intertwined with the development of movement. As a child's ability to move develops, the field of activity expands and so does the need for language.

From birth to 9 months

From birth, children turn their heads towards sources of sound, for example, the mouths of people speaking to them. By the end of this period, when they are sitting up, babies are babbling, and experimenting with first syllables.

From 9 months to 18 months

By nine months the instinctive grasping of the newborn has evolved into the intentional grasping of objects, accompanied by intentional sounds. The baby now knows that language is used to communicate, and understands what other people are saying. During this time the infant begins to crawl and to walk, and the first intentional words appear.

From 18 months to 2 years

Now walking without help, and with hands free to hold and manipulate as they go, the toddler explores every aspect of the environment, and learns a name for everything. Maximum effort is exerted as the toddler walks, lifts, carries and climbs. The child puts the same effort into language. Dr Montessori (1949/1982: 106) described this as the 'explosive epoch' of language development.

From 2 years

The child walks longer distances, and runs, climbs and hold things securely, the child's activity becoming increasingly purposeful and independent. At the same time the child's language becomes more secure, fluent and independent, and includes the emerging ability to talk about the future to guide purposeful, goal-directed activity.

The foundations of Montessori language education

The Montessori language programme is an extension of the two foundation areas of the Montessori approach:

- the exercises of practical life, in which children learn how to do everyday activities
- the exercises of the senses, in which children solve sensory puzzles.

Through these activities, children develop an orderly approach to their work. They learn to follow a given sequence, to manipulate objects with exactness and precision, and to self-correct. They also learn to concentrate, to attend to fine distinctions and to organize ideas in their mind for later retrieval and use. These accomplishments become the basis for the Montessori language learning activities, especially the activities for learning to write and to read.

The design of Montessori language materials

Language learning materials designed for young children are often brightly, but randomly, multicoloured, decorated with assorted child-oriented images such as animals, clowns or fantasy characters. Materials of this type encourage many diverse, often disconnected and non-systematic, uses. In comparison, the Montessori language materials can seem very plain, even austere.

- Each material has an exact use and a specific purpose.
- Every variation in texture, colour, shape, size or movement is related to that purpose.

In the Montessori view, any image or decoration unrelated to the educational purpose of the material has the potential to be distracting and confusing. It can also diminish the child's independence and creativity. If, for example, there is a picture of a koala on a box containing letters of the alphabet, children will need a teacher's help to turn their attention away from the koala to the letters, and the koala image has the potential to overshadow the children's own emerging ideas.

The Montessori language materials share features common to all Montessori materials.

- The materials are kept in perfect condition and placed in order on the shelf. Children choose work from the shelf and return it ready for the next person when they are finished.
- The materials are used with exactness and precision to capture interest, hold attention and build concentration.
- Abstract concepts are materialized in manipulable concrete objects. Children use their senses to perceive finer and finer distinctions. They are

given language to organize and hold these distinctions in their minds.

- There is a repertoire of exercises organized in incremental steps.
- Montessori teachers rehearse the movements and plan the exact placement of each object so that during a lesson, the relations between all the steps in a sequence and all the objects in an array are absolutely clear to the children.

Movement and manipulation are a feature of the way children use the Montessori language materials. For example, when they use the materials, children:

- trace with fingers and pencils
- walk with boxes, objects and labels to different parts of the room
- sort, match and sequence a variety of movable letters, cards, labels and objects
- act out and dramatize what they read
- tear apart and rearrange words written on strips of paper, combining them with movable objects and coloured symbols to create complex arrays.

Activity

Visit a library, school storeroom, educational retailer or anywhere you will find a collection of early childhood language education resources. Select three or four contrasting resources to review.
Consider the following questions:

1. What techniques are used to make the resource interesting for young children? Which of these techniques focus children's attention on the educational purpose of the resource? Which might be distracting?
2. How do children move when they use the resource? Do the movements relate to the educational purpose of the resource? Is there enough movement to satisfy the need for young children to be active?
3. Does the resource demand exactness and precision? Would the purpose be clear to children? Can children self-correct when using this resource? Can they work independently?

Spoken language

A child's urge to communicate with those around them, according to the Montessori tradition, drives the learning of language in early childhood. Children learn the language, or languages, they hear spoken around them during an extended sensitive period, which spans the first stage of development from birth to six years. From a Montessori point of view, the adult's task is not to work on children's language, but to help children develop themselves, in particular, to help children develop:

* know-how and independence, and therefore confidence in their own abilities
* knowledge about the world
* the ability to organize what is in the mind.

This development is indistinguishable from the development of language, because it is through language that children express their expanding understanding of the world.

Spoken language at home

Language surrounds a baby from birth. In the first months of a baby's life gestures, cries and babbling, even if merely instinctive, are interpreted by family members and carers as communication. Delighted responses from loved ones encourage the baby to interact more and more. Babies soon develop their own special way of communicating very effectively with immediate family members, but this does not satisfy them for long.

At around one, children make their first attempts to use words in ways people beyond the immediate family can understand. As beguiling as these early approximations can be, Montessori educators advise parents and carers not to respond with 'baby-talk' but, instead, to talk to children in clear, straightforward language they will want to imitate. They also recommend that children have as much opportunity as possible to hear people in the environment talking to each other. From this time children are collecting words to label things and events, and from about 18 months they begin to combine these words in early sentences. By the age of two children can communicate with people beyond the family, and they begin the lifelong enterprise of expanding what they can do with language.

Spoken language in the Montessori Infant Community

Language is considered, by Montessori educators, to be central to an infant's development. For this reason, experience with language is integrated incidentally into the full range of activities in a Montessori Infant Community. Some activities are dedicated specifically to language enrichment.

Early childhood educators who work with infants will find much that is familiar in the Montessori language experiences described below. All these approaches can be adapted to any setting in which adults interact with very small children.

Incidental language experience

The Infant Community fosters language development in many incidental ways.

- Whenever an adult speaks to an infant, the adult drops down to the child's level so the adult and child are communicating face to face.
- The language used to interact with infants is always respectful. For example, the adult never mimics a child's developing talk, but responds with clear language expressing meanings the child can understand, and imitate if they wish.
- Whenever an adult needs to do something to a child, such as change a nappy or wipe a nose, the adult explains to the child what is about to happen before carrying out the action.
- The names for things in the environment remain constant. The word *mat*, for example, is not used interchangeably with the word *rug* to name the same object.
- Vocabulary enrichment is built into most activities. When children wash their hands, for example, the adult might give them words such as *cold* or *wet* to describe the feel of the water.

Language enrichment

Language enrichment in the Infant Community revolves around sets of related objects, often beautiful miniatures. There might be, for example, a basket of animals, a bowl of fruit or vegetables, an outfit of clothes, furniture for a room, or a collection of things to take to the beach (a ball, a bucket and spade, sunglasses, a towel). Over time, in a progressive series of activities, children work with increasingly abstract representations of these sets.

- Children learn the names of the objects two or three at a time in a three-period lesson. When children know the names of two or more sets of objects, they mix them up and sort them.
- Later children are given photographs of the objects in each set and they match the objects to their photographs.
- Children match the miniature objects to real things, for example, matching the miniature dog in the basket of animals to a real dog, or a miniature chair to a real chair.
- Finally, children match the object to non-identical illustrations, for example, the apple in the fruit basket might be matched to a non-identical drawing of an apple.

Spoken language in the Children's House

Spoken language in the Children's House extends the principles used in the

Infant Community. Enrichment of vocabulary and language training activities from the time children enter the Children's House prepare them for writing and reading. The Sound Game helps children distinguish individual sounds in preparation for writing and reading.

Reflection point 〰️

Many aspects of the vocabulary enrichment, language training and language games described below will be familiar to all early childhood educators. Some details, however, give the activities an orientation that is distinctively Montessorian. As you read through these activities, compare them with your own repertoire and look for ideas you might be able to adapt to early childhood settings where you plan to work.

Enrichment of vocabulary

In the Children's House children are given opportunities, very systematically, to learn the names of everything in the environment. Knowing the name of everything contributes to children's independence and freedom.

- The teacher plays naming games with small groups of the youngest children. These games can be very energetic. One child at a time is asked to find an object and to stand beside it, for example: 'Can you stand next to the door?' The names used are accurate, for example, children learn that when they fetch a mug, it is not the same as fetching a cup. Naming games might also be played in the garden and when looking at a picture on the wall or into an aquarium.
- Whenever children are presented with a new exercise, for example, an exercise in practical life, they are given its exact name, as well as the names of all the objects used in the exercise.
- During the exercises of the senses children learn very precise adjectives to describe qualities. These adjectives can then be added to the naming games, for example: 'Can you get me the *yellow* plate? Stand beside the *big* cupboard.'
- Naming games are extended so children are asked to do actions as well as to fetch objects. The contrast between names and actions is highlighted.

There are also vocabulary enrichment activities that revolve around collections of pictures. The pictures in each set are mounted on cards of the same size, and colour-coded to show they belong together.

- The sets include pictures of things in the children's environment, for example, sets of pictures of different types of fruit, furniture, buildings or transport. In small groups children talk about the pictures, identifying the ones they can name. A three-period lesson can be used to teach unfamiliar names. Later, the children mix two or more sets, beginning with the most contrasting sets (for example, *fruit* and *furniture*) and progressing to similar sets (*fruit* and *vegetables*). Cards are sorted so each set is laid out on its own mat, the colour-coding acting as control of error. The sets are changed regularly to keep them fresh and interesting.

- Before a child is presented with a practical life exercise, the teacher ensures the child knows the name of the objects used in the exercise. If needed, the child works with pictures of the objects organized into sets classified according to function. Picture sets related to the exercises of practical life might include cleaning and cooking equipment, cutlery and crockery, fruit and vegetables, clothing and furniture.

- Some picture sets prepare children for later learning, including, for example, pictures of different types of animals, musical instruments or tools. Some sets have a picture of an object on the front and inside pictures of the parts of that object, for example, the parts of a plant or a computer. These sets are usually introduced with real objects. For example, the names of the parts of a flower are introduced using a real flower before children work with pictures of the parts of a flower.

Language training

Children listen to different ways people use language, including stories, poems, letters and biographies. Here are some of the many diverse examples of language training children might experience in a Montessori Children's House.

- Young children are told stories about real people and things, perhaps initiated with a real object or photograph, for example, stories about people they know, famous people, or people from history, stories about the lives of animals, stories of where products such as milk or paper come from, the story of a train trip, a house being built or clothing being made.

- Letters are read out to children from family members or classmates who are travelling or who have moved away.

- Factual books are read aloud to the children. On our visit to a Children's House in Chapter 2, we heard the teacher reading out loud from a book about wombats.

- Children love rhythmic and rhyming language, so they sometimes listen to and memorize rhymes and poems, later perhaps reciting them in groups or acting them out.

- As children grow older, they become more adept at distinguishing between fact and fiction, and more interested in problem-solving and judging right from wrong. This is the time children are introduced to imaginative story-telling and the reading out loud of good quality children's literature. Longer stories are sometimes read out loud in serial form to older children who stay for a full day. While the teacher is reading, children can just listen, or choose quiet work, perhaps drawing, sewing or handwriting.

The question game

Formal, spoken rituals such as 'Show and Tell' are not part of the Montessori approach. Instead, children are encouraged to share important news or stories with the teacher and one or two classmates as a way of starting up a conversation. Children might create a display as a conversation starter, as we saw happen on our visit to the Children's House in Chapter 2.

The question game is played to show children how to take turns in a conversation, or how to tell a story to an audience. In this game the teacher's questions guide children's contributions. This game can be easily adapted to any early years setting. For example, the teacher might use questions such as the following to help a child tell a group of classmates about a special gift.

What is it?
What is it made of?
What does it do?
Who gave it to you?
Where did it come from?
When did you receive it?
How did it reach you?
How does it make you feel?

The sound game

The teacher asks a small group of children, first, to listen to a sound, for example the sound /p/, and then to say the sound for themselves. Care is taken to articulate the sound in isolation from other sounds.

The teacher next thinks, out loud, of words that use this sound, inviting the children to help. In early lessons children work with beginning sounds (paper; apple) but in later games they listen for sounds in median or final position (happy; top; hand). When children are familiar with single letter sounds, the game can be played with digraph sounds, as in, for example, shop, cushion, fish; owner, flown, pillow. This game is played with small groups every day.

In Montessori schools the sound game is varied in a variety of ways to match children's interests and skill level, often in the form of an *I Spy* game.

- For very young children the teacher might limit the game to two or three familiar objects placed in front of the children on the mat. Initially, objects are chosen so the names begin with contrasting sounds, for example, an apple, a dustpan and a box. The teacher asks the children to find something beginning with /b/, indicating the box if more help is needed.
- Later children can:
  - 'spy' objects from anywhere in the room or beyond
  - collect objects with names that begin, or end, with the same sound
  - think of things that are not visible.
- By the age of six children can create lists of all the words they can think of containing a particular sound, either a single sound or a digraph, in first, middle and final position of words. They can search for the words in books.

Children first experience language as a continuous stream of sound. Some spoken language activities show children how the sound stream can be played with, re-shaped, stretched and embroidered. This includes activities that draw children's attention to:

- patterns of sound, for example, in rhymes
- patterns of rhythm and intonation, for example, in songs and poems
- patterns of wording and structure, for example, in stories.

Through the sound game and its variations children learn to attend to and perceive individual sounds separately from the language stream, and to organize them in their mind, in much the same way as they organized the qualities perceived in the exercises of the senses.

Spoken language in the Montessori classroom for six- to nine-year-olds

On entering a Montessori classroom for children aged from six to nine years, a visitor is often greeted by a child confidently offering a chair, and perhaps a cup of tea or coffee. They may also observe children using spoken language to:

- organize their work for the week
- collaborate on projects in all areas of the curriculum
- hold a meeting to decide class rules and to discuss solutions to classroom problems
- rehearse a play, a speech or a poetry performance
- telephone to arrange a field trip.

Questions for discussion 🗣

Can you think of other spoken language skills that might contribute to children's independence during the first years of school?

Written language

Children learn spoken language unconsciously. In Montessori terms, they absorb it as they strive to communicate with the people around them at home and in their community. In contrast, children must make a conscious effort to learn the skills needed to control written language.

In Dr Montessori's time, learning to write and read at school was a misery for many children as they struggled with pens and ink and reading out loud, not to mention the punishments and the humiliation lying in wait for those 'who blotted their copybook' or stumbled over words in a reader. This approach clearly stifled children's interest and was often ineffective, especially for those who had not yet developed a sense of order, hand control or concentration.

To teach the street children in her first school how to read and write, Dr Montessori (1948/1967: 203) analysed the processes of writing and reading, separating the 'mechanics' of handwriting and 'sounding out' from the intellectual demands of written composition and reading. She then designed sequences of exercises and games matched to children's interests, a sequence in which children learn to write before they learn to read.

Writing in the Children's House

In the Children's House the Montessori 'keys' to the doorway of literacy are:

- sandpaper letters
- movable alphabets
- metal insets.

Using these 'keys', children learn how to:

- form letters
- match sounds to letters
- analyse the stream of spoken language for individual sounds
- compose written language
- control a pencil.

The children put the skills together in their own time.

Sandpaper letters

The sandpaper letters are at least 6 cm high, cut from very fine sandpaper and glued onto smooth, thick card with a wide margin around each letter. Vowels are on blue cards and consonants on pink. Ideally, sandpaper letters are cursive, cut out so they join up when placed next to each other, and in the style recommended by local education authorities often for much older children. Cursive letters are used for the following reasons:

- Children see adults using cursive writing so it is more interesting.
- Cursive letters do not 'mirror' each other, as, for example, 'b' and 'd' in print.
- The flowing movements of cursive writing are closer to the natural movements of a child's hand than the staccato straight lines and perfect circles of print.

Sandpaper letters are presented to one child at a time. Beginning with letters that interest the child the most, for example, the first letter of the child's name, the teacher presents three contrasting letters at a time, usually two consonants and a vowel. Before the lesson the child has:

- distinguished rough from smooth in the touch exercises
- traced around the insets in the geometry and botany cabinets
- played the sound game repeatedly.

The child is now shown how to trace each sandpaper letter in one smooth, slow movement, from the starting point to the exit, saying the sound as their fingers leave the exit. The card is held still with the non-dominant hand and the letter is traced with two fingers of the dominant hand. This flowing movement teaches the child the letter shape. A three-period lesson, with lots of movement and fun in the second period, helps the child remember the sound of each letter. The teacher keeps accurate records of the progress each child makes learning the letters and sounds.

Correspondence between each letter shape and its sound is reinforced in the child's mind during independent work and group games. Once a letter can be traced with confidence, it can be traced in different media, for example, in a sand tray, in the air or in finger-paint, but always accompanied by its sound. Other activities include:

- sewing around letter outlines on cards
- tracing sandpaper letters grouped according to how they are formed (for example, a, d, g, q) and glued between two lines on the same long card or chart
- tracing the letters with chalk on a variety of chalkboards, with and without lines.

In Montessori schools children rarely copy rows of the same letter. Instead they are encouraged to practise one letter at a time, after tracing the sandpaper letter or from memory, and erasing their attempts until they have made one they think is just right.

Children from three to three and a half are very interested in tracing the sandpaper letters and saying the matching sounds, so it is relatively easy and straightforward for them to learn all the letters and sounds this way. There is no need, for example, to mark starting points or exits on letters for children of this age. They 'absorb' each letter as a unity of sound and movement. The sensitive period for touch wanes after about the age of four, so a more active and varied approach is used for older children who need more practice with sound–letter correspondence and letter formation.

In English-speaking classrooms there is also a set of sandpaper digraphs, often called phonograms by Montessori educators. The two letters of each digraph, for example, *ai* or *sh*, are glued on green cards and joined so they can be traced in one movement. The full set includes digraphs for 16 key sounds. Some Montessori teachers introduce the digraphs at the same time as the single letters; others introduce the digraphs later.

Movable alphabet
Once children know the sounds and letter shapes of enough vowels and consonants, they are ready to write! The only barrier for such young children is the inability to control a pencil. This barrier is overcome in Montessori classrooms with a movable alphabet. On our visit to the Children's House in Chapter 2 we saw a child composing words on the mat using the cut-out letters of a movable alphabet.

The first movable alphabet the children use is made of letters exactly the same size and shape as the sandpaper letters, the vowels cut from blue card and the consonants from pink. At least ten copies of each letter are stored in a wooden box, one compartment per letter.

Children begin using the movable alphabet once they know the sounds and shapes of about ten sandpaper letters. The movable alphabet box is placed to the left of a mat. In the first lesson the teacher thinks of a familiar phonetically spelled word using letters the child knows, for example, *sun*, and analyses the word out loud to isolate each sound, *s-u-n*. Then the child helps the teacher find in the box a letter for each sound, joining the letters on the mat to compose the word. The mat is quickly filled with words the child knows, although at this stage the child is not able to read the words.

When children use the movable alphabet, they analyse and experiment with the sounds and words of their own language. From the start they recognize the significance of the letters of the alphabet in helping them to express their own ideas and thoughts. Children are most interested in this work between the ages of three and four, and often enjoy doing it with their friends.

To learn how to place letters on lines, the children are sometimes given lined mats. They put two fingers down to make a space between words. Eventually they work with smaller movable alphabets made of print letters in one colour only. As their skill and independence increases, they write two- and three-syllable words, words with blends and digraphs, and eventually word groups, sentences and stories.

Writing with the movable alphabet is a bridge to reading. At first children rarely read back what they write but as they notice, for example, older children reading their writing, they begin to decode it for themselves. Once children become aware that their writing can be read back, their attention is drawn to spelling conventions.

Four- and five-year-old children, the chatterboxes in the room, have so much they want to talk and write about that the movable alphabet can become unwieldy. When this time comes, work with the metal insets has ideally prepared them to switch, with comparative ease, to pencil and paper.

Once they have moved on to pencil and paper, children in Montessori schools often 'publish' their writing in little booklets, which they carefully illustrate and bind with ribbon. These little books become first readers for the authors and their friends. Children are encouraged to experiment with different types of writing: stories, poems and factual writing. For older children whose hand control is not ready for pencil and paper, there are movable alphabets with letters and punctuation marks printed on little cards. Each letter card turns over to reveal the capital letter.

Metal insets

Children learn to hold and control a pencil in exercises with metal insets. The metal insets are ten geometric shapes painted blue, the same size as the shapes in the geometry cabinet. The insets fit into square pink metal frames. Children are most interested in this work between the ages of three and four. First they are shown how to sit and how to hold the pencil. They then use the frames and insets as stencils, carefully placed on sheets of square paper cut the same size as the frames.

The children trace around the shapes with a coloured pencil in an anti-clockwise direction just as they traced around the shapes of the geometry cabinet with their fingers. When they remove the inset and frame, the children see that the pencil has left a double outline on the paper. The outline is then filled in with contrasting colours in vertical, parallel lines from left to right and top to bottom in one continuous movement. The metal inset work progresses, incrementally, demanding ever-increasing exactness and precision as children fill in the outlines with finer and finer lines and shading. By combining shapes and colours, children create evermore complex and beautiful designs. The work flows into visual arts and geometry.

When children are ready, they transfer their skill with a pencil to writing, forming the letters using movements learned with the sandpaper letters. They are encouraged to write in a variety of media, including crayons and pencils on unlined and lined paper in different colours and textures.

The metal insets are one of the most popular activities in the Children's House, in sharp contrast to the copybooks they replaced. In Montessori schools children never practise separate strokes, curves or hooks, before writing whole letters. Unlike the letters themselves, these marks have no significance in the wider culture, and so, in the Montessori view, will not capture children's interest.

Activity

Review a commercial resource marketed to parents or teachers as a means of introducing young children to the letters of the alphabet and the corresponding sounds.

- How does the resource make learning the sounds and shapes of letters interesting for young children?
- How does the resource teach letter formation?
- How does the resource teach pencil control?
- Do children experience the letters as part of meaningful language use equivalent to the way written language is used in the wider culture?
- Using insights from the Montessori approach, how might you adapt this resource to make it more effective?

The written question game

The question game used to help children shape their spoken language for specific purposes can also be used to guide children's writing in the Children's House and beyond. The questions will change with the type of writing and its purpose. The answers to the questions can be recorded so these become the raw material the child, in collaboration with the teacher, uses to draft their writing. Around the age of six, children are ready to think about how to structure their writing, for example, how to organize information for a piece of factual writing, or how to write a story with a beginning, middle and end.

Reading in the Children's House

When, from about four years, children begin to decode the words they have composed with the movable alphabet, they are ready for the Object Boxes.

The Object Boxes

There are two Object Boxes. These are usually beautifully decorated and contain a collection of delightful miniatures the children love. As children work with the boxes, they 'discover' they can read, so the boxes have a very special place in Montessori classrooms. The objects in Object Box 1 have names that are spelled phonetically (Table 6.1).

In Object Box 2, there is one object with a name that includes one of the digraphs, or 'phonograms', children learn with the green sandpaper letters (Table 6.2).

Word reading

In Montessori classrooms, when children first learn to read, they are not asked to read out loud. The magic of writing is that it communicates meaning without speaking! Reading aloud is a performance skill learned much later. Instead children read words that generate activity. When a word-reading activity is first introduced to a child, the teacher usually writes words in beautiful handwriting on slips of paper while the child is watching. When the child knows how to do an activity, printed cards in colour-coded sets are used for independent work. Often, however, children want to write their own labels and word cards. Word reading activities include:

- labelling objects in the environment, both movable objects that can be carried to a mat as well as labels to place on immovable objects
- labelling the qualities of the sensorial materials
- labelling the picture card sets used to enrich vocabulary
- reading cards and booklets for learning all the ways of spelling each of the key digraph sounds (e.g. ways of spelling the key sound <u>ai</u> – tr<u>ai</u>n, s<u>ay</u>, c<u>a</u>k<u>e</u>, v<u>ei</u>n)
- learning sight words (puzzle words in Montessori terms)
- acting out action words written on red cards
- using beautiful charts and two movable alphabets in different colours to explore words and their parts (e.g. compound words, plurals, word families, prefixes, suffixes).

These cards are never used as flashcards, or in ways that draw attention to what children cannot yet read. Instead children who need extra practice might, for example, be given words on cards to copy with the movable alphabet.

Table 6.1 Object Box 1

Pre-requisite	The child has worked with the moveable alphabet for about six months.
Description	A box of miniatures with names spelled phonetically (e.g. jug, hat, fan, dog).
	A set of printed labels, one for each object.
Age	About 4 years.
Exercise	1. Carry the box, a pencil and some slips of paper to the table.
	2. Invite the child to take each object out of the box carefully, name it and place it on the table.
	3. With the child watching, write, very slowly, a 'message' on a slip of paper using the same cursive style as the sandpaper letters. (The 'message' is the name of one of the objects.)
	4. Ask the child to 'discover' the object you are thinking about by sounding out the letters one after the other.
	5. If needed, help the child say the sounds 'a bit quicker' so they fuse together.
	6. When the name emerges, the child places the label beside the object. This is a special moment. The child has discovered the word in the teacher's head without the word being spoken!
	7. In the same way the child reads and labels all the objects.
	8. The child mixes the objects up and labels them again.
	9. Explain that the print labels are for independent work whenever the child chooses.
Progression of work	1. Change the objects in the box regularly to maintain interest and vary the challenge, including:
	– objects named with two and three syllable phonetic words (e.g. pumpkin)
	– words with blends and double letters (e.g. drum, egg).
	2. The child can search in books for words he or she can read.

Reading and movement

In her first schools, Dr Montessori (1912/1964: 303–6) observed that five-year-old emergent readers rarely chose to read books, but they loved to decode words written on slips of paper, not out loud, but to use them as motives for activity. The activity included labelling objects, actions and qualities in the classroom. Children loved to combine reading with movement. By observing the children's activity, Dr Montessori monitored their reading, adapting the words on the labels to the children's skill and interest. As a first step beyond word reading, she wrote, also on slips of paper, simple commands for children to act out, the commands becoming gradually longer and more challenging in both reading and movement. Children in Montessori schools today still love to read and act out these reading commands, and eventually to write their own.

Table 6.2 Object Box 2

Pre-requisite	The child has worked with Object Box 1.
Description	A box of miniatures with names spelled phonetically and one miniature with a name that includes a digraph (e.g. <u>sh</u>ell, tr<u>ai</u>n, to<u>y</u>, clo<u>th</u>).
	A set of printed labels, one for each object
	Two small movable alphabets in contrasting colours
	A little booklet of words containing the same digraph as the name of the object, where each word is written on a separate page and the letters of the digraph are written in red.
Age	About 4 years.
Exercise	1. Write labels for the objects, one at a time. The child matches the labels to the objects.
	2. Write the name with the digraph last, reminding the child, if needed, that the two letters of the 'phonogram' together make one new sound.
	3. Ask the child to think of another word with this sound.
	4. Use the two movable alphabets to compose the child's word. Compose the digraph in a contrasting colour (usually red).
	5. With the child, continue thinking of words that use the digraph. Compose each new word under the previous one so the two letters of the digraph are placed under the same letters in the word above. Let the child take over when ready.
	6. Explain that the print labels and the little booklet are for independent work whenever the child chooses.
Progression of work	The child is gradually introduced to all the key digraphs, leaving the Object Box behind when it becomes too easy.
	The child practises digraphs by, for example:
	– writing words with digraphs using two coloured pencils
	– searching in books for words with digraphs
	– writing labels with digraphs for objects in the environment
	– using the movable alphabet to compose words with the digraphs from memory
	– word building with digraphs.

Young children in Montessori classrooms are not forced to read books if they are not ready. They can choose books, if they wish, from a small library of good quality children's books, both fact and fiction, but there is no requirement to work through sets of graded readers. Instead, children are offered active and interesting ways for practising the different components of reading. They put these components together in their own time, sometimes in what Montessori teachers call an 'explosion' into literacy.

Case study

India has just turned five. She has been working with the Montessori keys to literacy alongside other children in her age group. The others were making steady progress, but for a long time India was making no visible gains, until suddenly, almost overnight, she was writing and reading fluently. Every day now at school India writes stories with the moveable alphabet and every day she reads books, often looking for puzzle words and words with favourite 'phonograms' as she reads. She is constantly reading at home too.

Grammar and reading fluency

The decoding of individual words is described by Montessori teachers as 'mechanical' reading. Children at this level are not necessarily ready to read whole books, although there may be some who can. To read books, children must interpret the meaning of 'logical language', the Montessori term for connected written text. This transition is typically made in Montessori schools between the ages of five and seven, around the time children move onto the classroom for six- to nine-year-olds. To prepare for the intellectual demands of reading books, children in Montessori schools learn grammar.

When children decode words on labels for objects (nouns), actions (verbs) and qualities (adjectives), they are already using grammar to help them read. This work flows into the Montessori grammar games. As children play these games, they continue to use slips of paper and lots of movement, but, this time, they explore how different types of words combine to create the patterns, and meanings, of written language. The study of grammar gives children a way to order and organize into text the large number of words they accumulate in the word reading exercises.

The function of words

The grammar work begins with a series of games in which children, from the age of about five, learn the work, or 'function', of each type of word. There are games to introduce each part of speech. During these games children discover the work of:

- the 'noun family' (articles, adjectives, nouns)
- the 'verb family' (verbs, adverbs, pronouns)
- the 'servant' words (conjunctions, prepositions)
- the (very entertaining) interjection.

They do not yet use technical terms (e.g. *noun*), but identify words and their function by asking questions such as 'Which word is the name of what I want?' Word combinations are written on slips of paper. Children use the slips of paper to:

- read and label chosen objects arranged in a mini-environment, such as a model farm or a dolls' house (e.g. the white horse, a broken chair)
- read and act out (e.g. clap loudly, frown angrily).

Children tear the slips of paper apart to experiment with word order, often with hilarious results, and then, after re-ordering the words, they label each one with a movable 'grammar symbol' to make visible the work it does.

Each grammar symbol, one for each part of speech, is a geometric shape varying in colour and size in a way which draws attention to the function of that type of word and its relation to other words. For example, large red circles symbolize the energy of verbs, contrasting strongly with the large black triangles used to symbolize the substantiveness of nouns. In the shadow of the verb are smaller orange circles to symbolize adverbs, while adjectives, part of the noun's family, are smaller blue triangles.

Echoing the way the movable alphabet helps children attend to the stream of sound in spoken language, the movable grammar symbols help children analyse the stream of meaning in written language. When the symbols are placed over a sequence of words, the grammar pattern becomes visible to the children.

Reading analysis

The grammar symbols evolve into movable wooden circles, triangles and arrows used for reading analysis. Sentences, often taken from favourite books, are written on strips of paper. Children read each sentence and search for its parts. The verb (for example, 'ran') is cut out of the sentence and placed on a red circle. Children use questions such as 'Who ran?' and 'Where did she run?' to find the other parts of the sentence. The sentence parts are arranged, with the wooden symbols, around the verb to show the work of each part of the sentence. Through this work children learn the typical patterns of, in this case, English sentences.

The full scope and sequence of the Montessori grammar for children requires much more space to describe than is available here. The grammar work is one of Dr Montessori's most interesting contributions to early childhood education because it bridges the distance, in an active playful way, between 'sounding out' and the fluent reading of books and other extended texts. Even if children beyond the age of five or six remain reluctant to read books, these games provide plenty of meaningful reading practice combined with movement and laughter. Then, when children do become interested in books, they have all the skills they need to interpret the meaning of written language with success and enjoyment. The grammar games also teach children how to talk and think about word patterns in ways that are very helpful as the writing and reading demands of school become more challenging. Grammar becomes, in Dr Montessori's (1918/1965b: 7), words, 'the amiable and indispensable help to the construction of connected discourse'.

Reading and writing in the Montessori classroom for six- to nine-year-olds

The writing and reading activities of the Children's House extend into the six-to-nine classroom. The activities are adapted and broadened, however, to match the changing intellect and interests of children after the age of six, including:

- an interest in the reason for things
- the ability to imagine times and places distant from their own
- the urge to collaborate on projects with their peers
- a need for variety
- an interest in ethics.

The story of writing

Soon after they arrive in the classroom for six- to nine-year-olds, children are told a fable, often called *The Story of the Ox and the House*. The fable is told imaginatively and with dramatic effect in recognition that children of this age learn best when using their imagination.

Children are asked to imagine the life of early humans who had no language, and to think about how spoken language might have been invented. Then, using pictures and maps, the teacher outlines how the first rock art evolved, via cuneiform and hieroglyphics, into the signs used by the Phoenicians, including aleph (ox) and beth (house), that have come down to us, thanks to the Greeks and the Romans, as our alphabet. (This version of the story is obviously oriented to children working with languages that use the Roman alphabet.)

If being able to speak makes us human, the children are told, being able to write makes us immortal. Writers and their readers share the same place in time and space, no matter how many centuries or how many kilometres separate them.

The story is designed to sow seeds of interest that children will follow up on their own, for example, researching the Greeks or the story of writing that uses a different script from their own (e.g. Chinese writing). The story is told as a fable to ignite a sense of gratitude to the countless unknown, but ingenious, humans from whom we have inherited this wonderful gift. The reverence for written language communicated in this story permeates the work children do in the classroom.

Building skill and expertise with written language

Children often leave the Children's House writing and reading with some fluency. These children perhaps cannot remember a time they could not read. Learning to read for children older than six, however, requires much greater effort and by this age children also carry a greater burden of expectation from family and community members.

For emergent and beginning writers and readers older than six, materials such as movable alphabets and chalk boards are still used, but more as teaching aids, because at this age children are less inclined to work with them independently. These children tend to read before they write, working through the early literacy materials in a much shorter time, with many more variations and in a much livelier and less systematic way.

Grammar-based reading games continue to be important early reading experiences in the 'six to nine' class, but with variations to make them more dynamic and interesting for older children. In their study of words and grammar, they begin to use technical terms (e.g. *antonym, synonym, subject, object, verb, noun, abstract noun, concrete noun*).

Case study 📁

Six-year-old Sam has recently made the transition into the 'six to nine' class. He began metal inset work relatively late and lacks confidence with pencil control. While many of his peers have let moveable alphabets go, on most days Sam uses a moveable alphabet to cover a mat, or two, with imaginative stories or factual information. Everyone in the room has to walk around his compositions carefully to avoid messing up the letters. To record Sam's progress with writing,

(Continued)

(Continued)

the teacher photographs each finished piece before he puts the letters away. One day Sam has to share the last available alphabet box with someone else. The writing is not finished when the letters run out. Sam fetches paper, pencil and a writing stool and finishes the work. He also draws a picture. He places the end of his story, and the illustration, on paper as a continuation of the letters on the mat, and the teacher takes a photo as usual. Then Sam says: 'No more photos!' From now on, all his writing is on paper that can go directly into his portfolio.

Not long after that Sam starts to write a 'chapter' book on the computer with a friend. An older child shows them how to use the typing program to improve their keyboard skills. The teacher uses a variation of the written question game to help them structure their story. It is a big work, taking many days to draft, edit and proofread, but the finished book, illustrated and bound, soon becomes a class favourite.

Grammar boxes

Seven- and eight-year-old children use the Montessori grammar boxes to explore variation in word patterns and the meanings they make. The grammar boxes are a series of colour-coded boxes, each with a large compartment for reading cards plus smaller compartments for individual words on small cards colour-coded according to function. Children read the text on the large cards, for example:

- Smooth the paper.
- Crumple the paper.

They act out both combinations of words to experience the difference in meaning. They use the colour-coded individual words to reconstruct the text and place grammar symbols over the reconstructed text to make the grammar pattern even more visible.

Written language as a resource for learning and creating

A small library enables children to research topics of interest and to enjoy a wide range of literature. As their reading becomes more secure, interest in writing gathers speed again, this time as a tool for:

- communication with others (e.g. messages, letters)
- organizing and displaying the results of research (e.g. project work, displays)

- creative expression (e.g. stories, poems, plays, calligraphy)
- personal and critical responses (e.g. to rules, advertising, books, films).

Computers are a further aid to research, composition and publication.

Case study

The state education authority required all children in Year 3 to sit a literacy test. The children in the third year of the Montessori class for six to nine year olds had never completed a literacy worksheet or a writing test before. They were shown how to do a literacy test as an exercise in practical life. There was then a discussion in which the children:

- talked about why people in their society think it is important for children of their age to know certain things and to have certain skills
- planned how they would fill in any gaps in their knowledge and skill.

On the day of the test, the children enjoyed the novelty of the exercise, but later decided the work they do in class with their friends is more interesting and challenging.

Since 1907, when the unlikely children in Dr Montessori's first school in Rome suddenly 'exploded' into writing, her method has been adapted for children from many different language backgrounds, some from literate backgrounds and some for whom literacy is not part of daily life. The extensive repertoire of exercises and games supports children who need more time to learn to write and read, while early writers and readers advance at their own pace. In bilingual and multilingual classrooms the materials are duplicated for each language spoken in the classroom.

Summary

This chapter has provided an overview of Montessori language education. It introduced the Montessori view of the interrelation between language development and the development of movement as well as the distinctive design features of the Montessori language materials. A selection of exercises and games illustrated the Montessori approach to the development of both spoken and written language in early childhood.

Things to think about

- What is the relation between the development of movement and the development of language in early childhood?
- What is the relation between spoken and written language in early childhood?
- Review the literacy skills and concepts a child encounters in a Montessori early childhood setting. How do these compare with other early childhood literacy programmes?
- What are the key points of difference between the Montessori approach to the teaching of reading and the teaching of reading in other early childhood reading programmes with which you are familiar? What might be the advantages, and disadvantages, of the Montessori approach?

7

Montessori mathematics

Chapter objectives

- To explore how mathematics education in Montessori early childhood settings builds on the foundation exercises of practical life and the senses.
- To highlight the distinctive design features of the Montessori mathematics materials.
- To provide an overview of the Montessori mathematics curriculum from early childhood to the school years.
- To explore 'the passage to abstraction' as the organizing principle of the Montessori mathematics curriculum.

Dr Montessori loved mathematics. As a young girl in Italy in the 1880s she chose to attend a boys' technical school just so she could study mathematics. This love of mathematics is very visible in the wonderful materials she designed so young children could share her enthusiasm. In the Montessori view the 'mathematical mind' is a manifestation of several human tendencies.

- Humans are driven to explore and to investigate their environment. To do this effectively, they need to orient themselves in an ordered way.
- Humans think about things that are not immediately present to the senses, in other words, they imagine. The raw material for their imagination is abstraction, the mental organization and ordering of ideas that can be retrieved at a later time. Abstract ideas become the basis for reasoning and judgement.
- From ancient times to the present, and in all parts of the world, human beings have calculated and measured things.

If these tendencies are shared by all humans, then all children should enjoy mathematics, and do well at it. With this in mind, Dr Montessori designed an array of intriguing objects that materialize abstract mathematical concepts. Children in Montessori schools first experience mathematical concepts represented in the form of concrete objects. After repeatedly manipulating and rearranging the objects materializing a concept, children, in their own time, construct the corresponding abstract concept for themselves.

Too many people leave school believing maths is an impenetrable subject accessible only to a select few. A feature of Montessori mathematics materials is the way they transform a mathematical process, even one with a reputation for being difficult, so it becomes both accessible and fascinating. During Montessori teacher training courses many people are astounded to discover they can become completely absorbed in the finer points of, for example, long division, multiples and square roots.

Case study 🗀

An early childhood teacher, having worked in a Montessori Children's House for several years, tells her colleagues: 'What continues to amaze me is the joy of mathematics in Montessori!'

Reflection point 〰

Why do you think so many students learn to think of mathematics as difficult? What can early childhood educators do to address this problem?

The foundations of Montessori mathematics education

The study of mathematics in a Montessori classroom, like the study of language, is built on the foundation exercises of practical life and the senses.

- Through the exercises of practical life children learn about order and sequence, and how to use even the smallest objects, with precision and accuracy. They also learn to concentrate.
- Through the exercises of the senses children learn to compare and contrast, to perceive fine distinctions and to construct abstract ideas from concrete experience.
- The sensorial materials also prepare children for work with a wide range

of mathematical concepts, including dimension, length, mass and volume. Working with objects in sets of ten prepares children for working with a mathematical system based on ten.

The design of the Montessori mathematics materials

When children use the Montessori mathematics materials, they explore mathematical concepts using movement and their senses. Since Dr Montessori's time, and perhaps in part thanks to her pioneering work, this idea has become commonplace in many early childhood settings. Young children in early childhood settings everywhere are introduced to mathematics through play-like activity with concrete materials. There is an abundance of novel resources available in a variety of colours, textures, sizes and shapes. Many have multiple uses and are valued for their imaginative possibilities. Beside this array, the Montessori mathematics materials, just like the Montessori language materials, can seem a little austere and inflexible.

Dr Montessori (1912/1964; 110–11) was very critical of educators who try to interest children with irrelevant and distracting decoration and activity. After observing a lesson in which little cardboard dancers were used to teach addition, she comments:

> If *I* remember the dancers more clearly than I do the arithmetic process, how must it have been with the children?

In Dr Montessori's view, if children are shown how to use, in an exact way, concrete materials designed to precise specifications, they will:

• stay interested and maintain concentration
• focus their attention on the concept they are learning.

An extension of the sensorial materials
The design of the Montessori mathematics materials echoes and augments the distinctive features of the sensorial materials.

• Each set of objects materializes a single concept or process in a concrete form which children can explore with their senses. Every variation in quantity, colour, shape or size contributes to the materialization of the concept. The design foreshadows concepts and relations children will encounter in their future study of mathematics.
• The objects are aesthetically appealing. They are kept in perfect condition. Children are shown how to return the work to the shelf so it is ready for the next person. Sets with broken or missing objects are removed from the classroom.

- The objects encourage independent use.
- There is a limited number of each set of objects to encourage children to use them with respect and care.
- Each set of objects is used in a very precise way related to the concept being taught. This limits confusion and distraction, encourages concentration and makes the activity more interesting.
- The design enables the child to self-correct.

Multiple layers of representation

One of the most distinctive features of the sets of Montessori mathematics materials is the way the same element of mathematical knowledge is represented simultaneously, and very exactly, in multiple ways, for example:

- in the shape, colour and size of objects
- in the movements used to manipulate the objects
- in the way the objects are laid out at the conclusion of an exercise
- in the language used to talk about the objects and their use
- in the mathematical symbols used to represent the concept embodied in the objects.

Knowledge represented in so many ways at the same time carries more 'weight' and has a greater chance of leaving an impression on children's minds. This impression becomes the foundation on which children construct an abstract representation of the concept in their minds. Montessori teachers know children are making the 'passage to abstraction', as it is called in the Montessori tradition, when they begin to 'let the materials go'; in other words, when the over-representation becomes more of a hindrance than a help. Once the knowledge has been transformed to an abstraction held in the mind, it becomes easier to work with the concept without the concrete materials. This is one of the mathematical secrets children discover in Montessori classrooms!

Case study 🗁

When asked which part of her work she enjoys the most, a Montessori teacher in a 'six to nine' classroom says it is when children rush up, bubbling over with excitement to tell her: 'I did it all by myself and I didn't even need the materials!'

The passage to abstraction

The Montessori mathematics curriculum from the Children's House through to the first years of school comprises a vast repertoire of exercises and games. These exercises and games relate to sets of concrete objects that embody mathematical concepts. The concrete materials introduce children to whole numbers and fractions, as well as to geometry and measurement, from many different perspectives. The work often involves using the objects for problem solving or research. The exercises are progressive, each one contributing incrementally to the child's construction of mathematical knowledge.

The first exercises in a series introduce new concepts through work with the concrete objects. Follow-up activities repeat and reinforce the concept, leading the child, one step at a time, towards holding the concept in the mind, in other words, leading the child to abstraction. The teacher never takes short cuts on this path, but children often discover short cuts on their own and make progress in leaps and bounds in their own time following their own interests. Once children have grasped a concept abstractly, the concrete material is left behind.

Case study 🗁

Clara and Georgina are between five and six years old. On our visit to the Children's House in Chapter 2 we see them skip-counting a chain of beads stretched out along the floor. This chain is one of a series of colour-coded chains stored together in a wooden cabinet, along with matching colour-coded squares and cubes made out of beads. In the cabinet are ten short chains children use to count to the square of each number from 1 to 10, and ten long chains for counting to the cube of each number. As the girls work, the sequence of numbers is increasingly etched in their mind, numbers they will later encounter as products, multiples, squares and cubes.

Indirect preparation in a spiral curriculum

Many materials introduced to young children reappear later in the curriculum. The short chain of four in the chain cabinet, for example, is yellow. The beads are organized on the chain in four sets of four bars, each bar made of four beads. Children use the chain to skip-count by fours to 16, labelling as they count each multiple of four with its number on a little yellow arrow. They also fold the chain so the bead bars are lined up to make a square, which they match to a yellow square of 16 beads.

The long chain of four is also yellow and bars of four beads are again grouped in fours, but this time the length of the chain is equivalent to four short chains. Children use this chain to skip count and label multiples of four up to 64. The long chain is folded and matched to four squares of 16 beads. These squares can be piled on top of each other and matched with a cube made out of 64 beads.

The first chains the children work with are the short and long chains of ten. These chains are called, respectively, the hundred chain and the thousand chain. The beads are gold in colour. By the time children reach this work, they know the quantity one hundred as a square of one hundred golden beads and the quantity one thousand as a cube of one thousand golden beads. In this work they see the quantities stretched out in a line. Children often cannot wait until they count the thousand chain. Younger children watch in awe, and step carefully, as older children stretch this beautiful chain of golden beads the full length of the classroom and begin the big work of counting it and labelling it, by tens, all the way to one thousand.

In the Children's House the chains are used in counting games. In the 'six to nine' classroom, children use the chains to help them memorize multiplication number facts and to work with multiples. In the classroom for children aged from 9 to 12, the chains are used to learn about the powers of numbers.

Mathematics in everyday life

Ideally, in early childhood, shared mathematical experiences are as much a part of everyday life as, for example, shared reading experiences, if children are not to think of maths as something that only belongs at school. There are books and Internet sites with many ideas for how this might be done. From the Montessori perspective, everyday activities are a rich source of mathematical experiences that contribute to children's independence both in the Infant Community and in the Children's House. In the Montessori Infant Community, for example, children set their own place at the table. The shape of each item of cutlery, as well as of a plate and a cup, is embroidered onto the place mat. Infants set their place by matching the objects to the embroidered outlines.

Here are some other examples that can be adapted for any age group in the early years.

- Mathematics can be used to achieve practical purposes, for example:
  – ensuring cutlery or clothing correspond to the number of family members when setting the table or folding laundry, adding extra places when

there are guests and counting in pairs to match socks
   – counting how many people can fit in the car, how many sleeps before
     an important event or how many hooks are needed for all our hats and
     coats
   – estimating how long we still have to travel or the box size needed to
     store all the toys
- Mathematics can be used to build harmonious social relations (grace and
  courtesy), for example:
   – sharing (turns, toys, food or space)
   – punctuality (when to arrive, when to leave)
   – routines (getting up, mealtimes, school times, playtime, television, bed-
     time)
- Mathematics can be used for fun, for example:
   – counting how many seconds you can stare or stand completely still on
     one foot
   – estimating and measuring how far you can swim, throw or kick a ball,
     or how fast you can run a given distance
   – counting steps, skips and hops, and measuring jumps
- Mathematical language can be used when:
   – measuring solid and liquid ingredients for food preparation
   – identifying objects (the circular table, the kilogram weight)
   – choosing (square plate or circular plate, a deep bath or a shallow bath,
     1m of ribbon or 30 cm of ribbon)
   – learning about the body (how many eyes, ears, legs, fingers, toes, etc;
     how often do you blink or how many heartbeats in a given time; mak-
     ing a height chart).

Reflection point 〰

Can you think of other ways to use mathematical ideas in everyday life to help
young children become more independent?

Mathematics in the Children's House

Work with the mathematics materials in the Children's House begins
around the age of four, after children have spent a year or two working with
the exercises of practical life and the senses. This foundation ensures they
can work with the mathematics materials independently and successfully.
Ideally, children are also making good progress with the language materials
before the mathematics work starts. One reason for this is that the
Montessori mathematics materials are so enticing and numerous, there is a

risk the language work will be overshadowed if it is not well established first.

Numbers to ten

Our counting system is based on 10. If you can count to 10, and you understand the concept of zero, you have the key to the whole base 10 number system.

Children in Montessori schools work with multiple representations of the base 10 system of numbers. The work begins, when children are about four, with the following exercises and games. For children who already know something about the numbers to 10 before they start this work, the following exercises help them organize what they know in an ordered way so they can retrieve it later.

Number rods

The 10 number rods are the same size and shape as the 10 red rods children used in the sense exercise in which they built a stair from the longest rod, 1 m in length, to the shortest, 10 cm in length. The number rods, however, are painted in alternating red and blue segments, each segment the same length as the shortest rod that now represents the quantity one. The rod for one is red. The rod for two has one blue and one red segment, and so on, up to the rod for 10, with 10 segments of alternating colour.

Beginning with one, children count the segments on each rod, and build the stair. In this way they gain an impression of each quantity as an entity in its own right and in relation to the other quantities. A three-period lesson is used to teach the names of the quantities.

To teach children the numerals, sandpaper numbers are used in the same way as sandpaper letters. When the children have learned the quantities and the numerals separately, they put them together by matching number cards to the rods representing the quantities.

Reflection point 〰

This same pattern is used throughout the Montessori maths curriculum. Children experience quantities in concrete form first, then they learn the symbols and finally they match symbol to quantity.

Spindle boxes

There are nine spindle boxes each labelled with a numeral from 0 to 9. Children count out the number of long wooden spindles for each numeral, tie the spindles into a bundle and place the bundle in the correct box. This time they experience each quantity as collections of units and the empty box as zero. They also experience nine as a counting limit, in preparation for nine always being the limit before the transition to the next hierarchy of the number system.

Cards and counters

The children place number cards from 1 to 10 in sequence. From a collection of 55 green counters they then count out the matching quantity and place it under each card, until no counters are left. The counters are arranged two by two in a column, with the last counter under each odd number placed in the middle of the column. This gives children a first impression of odd and even numbers.

Memory game of numbers

This is the first group game in mathematics. Each number, from 0 to 10, is written on a piece of paper. The paper is folded and placed in a basket. Taking turns, children draw out numbers and fetch that number of identical objects from the environment, for example, two baskets, five cups, eight leaves. The child who draws zero very obviously fetches nothing. While this game is fun, it also tests whether the children have abstracted the quantities in their minds and can transfer this knowledge to different aspects of the environment.

Discussion point

Children in Montessori schools experience mathematical concepts, for example, the quantities from 0 to 10, as materialized abstractions before they apply them to objects in their environment.

How does this learning sequence compare with the way children are introduced to the numbers one to ten in other early childhood settings?

The Decimal System

The work with numbers to 10 gives children the key to the world of numbers. They are now ready to explore the whole system using some of the most beautiful materials in the Montessori environment, the golden beads.

The golden beads materialize four hierarchies of the decimal system:

- a single, loose golden-coloured bead represents a unit
- ten golden beads wired together to form a bar represents a ten
- ten golden ten-bars wired together to form a square represents a hundred
- ten golden hundred-squares wired together to form a cube represents a thousand.

The original golden beads are made out of sparkling glass, the golden colour indicating how valuable the decimal system is in our culture. Not only is the relative value of each hierarchy represented in the quantity of beads, but also in volume and mass. Many classrooms keep one special set of glass beads, but when larger quantities of material are needed, plastic beads are used. Extra hundred-squares and thousand-cubes are also made out of wood.

This material was originally designed for eight-year-olds, but Dr Montessori observed that four- and five-year-olds were attracted to it most.

Exercises with the golden beads are usually done in small groups. The children manipulate each quantity and learn its name in a three-period lesson. In a separate three-period lesson children learn the names for symbols printed on cards:

- the units, from one to nine, are printed in green on small square cards
- the tens, from 10 to 90, are printed in blue on cards twice the length of the unit cards
- the hundreds, from 100 to 900, are printed in red on cards three times the length of the unit cards
- the thousands, from 1000 to 9000, are printed in green on cards four times the length of the unit cards.

During the lesson the children count the number of zeros on the card to discover the tens have one zero, hundreds have two zeros and thousands have three zeros.

The children put the quantities together to make an array of beads and cards. They learn to fetch, in a tray from a 'bank' of golden bead material, a quantity such as two thousands, five hundreds, three tens and six units in both material and cards. By placing the numbers on the cards in order, one on top of the other, with the thousand card on the bottom, and sliding all the cards to the right, they discover 'the magic' of place value. The zeros disappear to reveal the four colour-coded hierarchies represented as one four-digit number, in this case, 2536. The children use this number to label the quantity represented in beads.

Case study

In the Children's House there has been a recent surge in interest in work with the golden beads. Harry, who is four, has been watching this flurry of activity with fascination. At last it is his turn to start the golden bead work himself. His observation of the other children in previous weeks has prepared him. He is already familiar with the use of the material even before his first lesson. In the morning Harry can't wait to start. Before he enters the classroom or puts his things away, he calls out: 'Let's do golden beads!' The first thing he does is set up the big array of beads and cards all by himself.

Over a period of at least a year, in the Children's House and the 'six to nine' class, children use the golden beads in a series of exercises through which they explore the workings of the decimal system. For example, to practise trading with the golden beads, children play the change game in the following way:

- They fill a tray with random quantities of units, tens, hundreds and thousands, inevitably collecting more than ten of at least one category. The quantities are placed on a mat in a 'big mess'.
- To sort out the mess, children count the quantities, hierarchy by hierarchy, beginning with the units. They call out 'Stop!' when they have 10 of any quantity, before going to the 'bank' to exchange the 10 for one of the next hierarchy.
- When they have sorted out the mess, they count how much of each quantity they have left on the mat and fetch number cards to match. They put the number cards together and slide them to hide the zeros, before placing the number in front of the series of quantities.

Working in groups of three, children use the golden beads to enact the four operations with quantities and matching number cards to four digits:

- To enact addition, children collect quantities in bead material with matching cards, put the material all together 'in a mess', sort the material into hierarchies and count the total, changing as needed, then labelling the result with number cards.
- To enact subtraction, children collect a 'big' quantity and take a smaller quantity away, then count and label the difference left behind.
- To enact multiplication, children add the same quantity a certain number of times to experience multiplication as a special kind of addition.
- To enact division, children share a 'big' quantity equally so each person receives the same. Then they label the amount one person receives.

In the 'six to nine' classroom children are taught the names for the parts of these operations (e.g. sum, difference, product, quotient). When the golden bead material becomes too cumbersome and slows them down too much, children continue the work with the stamp game. In this game the quantities are represented in little identical square tiles that vary in colour according to the hierarchy:

- green units
- blue tens
- red hundreds
- green thousands, i.e. units of the next hierarchial 'family', the family of thousands.

The stamp game is the first step towards the 'passage to abstraction'. As children progress through the mathematics curriculum, from now on probably in the 'six to nine' classroom, the colour coding of the decimal system hierarchies remains constant, repeatedly revealing the underlying pattern of the number system. This colour coding recurs in the following materials:

- bead frames children use to guide them as they progress to calculation with symbols only
- materials representing quantities in the thousands family (green 'units of' thousands, blue tens of thousands and red hundreds of thousands) and the millions family (green 'units of' millions, blue tens of millions, red hundreds of millions)
- materials representing decimal fractions (blue tenths, red hundredths, green thousandths)
- in concrete materials used for long multiplication and long division calculations.

When children have completed the decimal system work, and all the parallel exercises, they have a very solid and sophisticated understanding of the base ten number system and how it works.

Case study 🗀

In a Montessori 'six-to-nine' classroom Rebecca and Jana, both aged about eight, are totally absorbed in using coloured beads, little cards and the Montessori checkerboard to solve long multiplication problems involving six-digit numbers. These are problems they have invented for themselves. They use calculators to check their solutions.

Reflection point 〰

Montessori teachers sometimes create parallel materials to show children, usually older than nine, how to count and calculate in number bases other than ten. For example, they might show children how to count in base five in which four is the limit before changing to the next hierarchy. Children might also research base two, the binary system so important to electronic technology but also the system used by indigenous Australians for millennia, or base 60, the system used in ancient Mesopotamia that we remember whenever we tell the time or measure angles.

   Learning to count in a base other than base ten is a useful experience for teachers, too. The challenge an adult faces learning to count in base eight, for example, is comparable to the challenge small children face when they first learn to count in base ten.

Parallel games and exercises

Parallel to work with the hierarchies of the decimal system, children encounter sets of concrete materials representing the same quantities in new ways, opening up new possibilities for working with numbers and number patterns.

- The quantities 1 to 10 are represented as a stair of bead bars, each a different colour. The longest bead bar, the base of the stair, is 10, the golden 10-bar the children already know. The smallest bead bar is one, a single red bead. These bead bars are used in a series of activities in which children learn the teen quantities and quantities to one hundred, with corresponding symbols. This work is extended to linear counting and skip counting with the chains.
- Children discover number facts for themselves using concrete, manipulable material, a different set of material for each operation. They then embark on a long series of varied activities through which, over time, they gradually memorize these facts. These exercises also include first experiences in algebraic reasoning. Knowing the number facts makes the passage to abstraction possible.

Case study 📁

The teacher is presenting five-year-old Lachlan with the multiplication board for the first time. The multiplication board is a wooden board with a square array of 100 indentations. Children count groups of beads into the indentations to

(Continued)

(Continued)

make products, discovering the multiplication table for themselves, recording the products in a special booklet. When Lachlan saw the board with all 100 beads in place (10 x 10), he ran off and came back with a 100-square made of golden beads.

Reflection point 〰

There are a countless connections and comparisons to be made between elements of the Montessori mathematics curriculum. Children are always discovering these connections for themselves. These are often real 'eureka' moments. The mathematical knowledge children gain from working with the Montessori materials is also connected with everyday life, most notably through measurement in all its forms.

Working with fractions

The Montessori fraction material shows children, in concrete form, that there are quantities smaller than the unit. This material is a series of ten green square metal frames, each one with a red circle inset. The red circle is the red unit bead flattened out. The first circle in the series is a whole, the second is divided into two equal pieces, and so on, until the final circle is divided into ten equal pieces. Children first experience these quantities as puzzle pieces. They are later given the names of the fractions, and discover, with concrete materials, they can do the same operations with these quantities as they do with the whole numbers.

Mathematics in the classroom for six- to nine-year-olds

When children move from the Children's House to the classroom for six- to nine-year-olds, they continue working through the mathematics exercises and games. Children might be working anywhere along the spectrum, from numbers to 10, the golden beads, the parallel games or the materials leading to abstraction, but now they advance more rapidly and in a much more energetic way. Work with fractions also continues and gradually progresses to decimal fractions.

While younger children are happy to repeat exercises, from the age of six children enjoy novelty, so the teacher draws on an expanded repertoire of many variations for each material, until children are ready to let that particular material go. The variations are extremely diverse, often involving experimentation, research and the creation of charts or models. The lessons are much more high-spirited, often involving dramatic representation or story-telling.

The concrete materials are used in the Children's House to give children impressions of a whole range of mathematical concepts. In the 'six to nine' classroom, lessons are much more explicit and children's impressions are transformed into conscious knowledge. For example, when children first arrive in the 'six to nine' classroom, the cards and counters exercise is sometimes used to review their knowledge of the numbers to ten. During this exercise, to add novelty and interest, they are now taught explicitly about odd and even numbers, something they had only gained an impression of in the Children's House.

The story of numbers

Just as children are told the story of the writing system, soon after they enter the 'six-to-nine' classroom they are also told the story of numbers. In the same imaginative and entertaining way children are told how the numbers we use today have come to us from India via the Middle East. Zero was invented in India and its impact is highlighted, for example, by looking at the numerals used by the Ancient Romans, which lack a zero, and comparing them with the flexibility of our number system. This 'great' story often sparks children's interest in exploring the use of numbers in other parts of the world. Just like the letters of the alphabet, numbers are presented as a wonderful gift we have inherited from humans who have gone before. Similarly, children are told the history of the measurement systems we use in our culture as an introduction to the study of measurement.

Activity

Base 10 blocks have been used widely in early childhood settings for many years. These blocks, designed by Dr Zoltan Dienes, are modelled on the Montessori golden beads.
1. Answer the following questions based on your own experience or research.
2. At what age do children use the base 10 blocks?
3. Are they used in the same ways as the Montessori golden bead material?
4. How does their use differ?

Geometry

The study of geometry is a feature of Montessori classrooms for children from the age of six. There is a particularly rich array of concrete materials used in an extensive sequence of lessons, exercises and games.

In the Children's House, geometry is said to be 'hidden' in sensorial materials such as the geometry solids, the geometry cabinet and the constructive triangles. Children learn to recognize shapes through sight, touch and movement and they learn to name them in three-period lessons.

In the Montessori 'six to nine' classroom, geometry becomes a domain of knowledge studied in its own right. Children continue to work with the same set of materials, but now, as each shape is introduced and as part of the three-period lesson, the teacher tells a story based on the etymology of the name. For example, while emphasizing the sharpness of the three corners of a triangle, the teacher will explain the etymology of the name 'triangle' (tri – three; angle – corner). In this way children learn names of the shapes in classified sets, for example, sets of triangles (e.g. scalene, isosceles, equilateral), quadrilaterals (e.g. square, rectangle, parallelogram, trapezium, rhombus) and regular polygons (e.g. pentagon, hexagon etc).

Instead of playing memory games with geometry shapes, as in the sense exercises, older children choose follow-up work from a set of 'command cards' with suggestions for a variety of activities involving, for example, labelling, matching, sorting, looking for shapes in the environment, making models of solid shapes, and drawing, cutting and gluing activities with shapes.

Once children can recognize and name sets of shapes, they begin the task of analysing those shapes using the box of Montessori geometry sticks. The 'box of sticks' contains colour-coded, flat, wooden sticks, calibrated in units from one to ten. Using these sticks, and other objects in the box, children construct different types of lines, angles, polygons and closed curves, and analyse their parts. They take several years to complete all the exercises. Accompanying the concrete materials is a series of booklets with illustrations, labels and definitions as well as sets of command cards. The booklets act as a control of error and the command cards suggest activities in which children apply what they have learned. In this way, through their own activity, children progress steadily to an abstract understanding of geometry concepts.

Discussion point 🗨 👥

How is knowledge about geometry incorporated into early childhood settings with which you are familiar? How does this differ from the Montessori approach? How is it the same?

What do you think is the value of geometry in early childhood education?

Mathematics as a prepared path to culture

The description of the complete array of Montessori mathematics materials and exercises was first published in Spain in 1934 Montessori (1971, 1934 in Spanish). It filled two volumes: *Psicoaritmética* and *Psicogeométria*. Why did Dr Montessori use the intriguing prefix 'psico' to describe her mathematics pedagogy?

The first reason is that the pedagogy is designed to match the special psychology of children, first children under six, who explore with their senses and think with their hands, and then later, further along the path to mathematical culture, children over six, who think with their imagination, and who are moving along the passage to abstraction.

The second reason is that the pedagogy has the potential to change children's consciousness by changing what they pay attention to and what they are able to perceive. It draws their attention to distinctions, patterns and relationships they would not otherwise be able to see in ways that are meaningful in the field of mathematics as it is understood in the children's culture. Mathematics then becomes, not a collection of dry and difficult facts, but a powerful intellectual and cultural tool.

Summary ▢

This chapter is an overview of Montessori mathematics education. It showed how mathematics is an extension of the foundation exercises of practical life and the senses, and reviewed the distinctive design features of the Montessori mathematics materials. A synopsis of the Montessori mathematics curriculum highlighted 'the passage to abstraction' as an organizing principle.

Things to think about

In the Montessori mathematics curriculum children are introduced to concepts in the following sequence:

1. materialized quantity
2. manipulable symbol
3. labelling quantity with symbol
4. exploring different ways of working with concrete quantities and manipulable symbols
5. passage to abstraction
6. transfer of the concept to applications in the wider environment.

Review an early childhood mathematics programme with which you are familiar. Consider how the programme introduces children to mathematical concepts and skills such as the following:

• counting whole numbers
• place value
• addition and subtraction
• multiplication and division
• number facts
• fractions
• algebraic reasoning
• measurement.

Compare the sequence of lessons in this programme with the Montessori approach, with particular reference to:

• the role of concrete materials
• the role of movement, manipulation and construction
• the use of mathematical symbols
• the abstract and applied use of mathematical concepts
• the role of dramatic play and story-telling.

What insights have you gained from the Montessori approach to mathematics in early childhood that you can apply to your own practice?

Prepared paths to culture

Chapter objectives

- To review Montessori prepared paths to culture in the fields of science, geography, history and the visual arts.
- To discuss the use of specialist and technical terms in Montessori early childhood education.
- To explore the Montessori approach to education for peace and sustainability.

Dr Montessori worked on her pedagogy during the first half of the twentieth century. The turmoil in Europe over those decades inevitably shaped her work. After World War I the Montessori method was adapted to meet the needs of child refugees. By the 1930s, Europe was again descending into war. All Montessori schools in Italy were closed, Montessori books were burned in Berlin and the Montessori family were forced from their home in Barcelona. During this time Dr Montessori spoke at peace conferences across Europe, arguing that the only way to solve the problem of war was to educate children for peace. With this in mind, Dr Montessori designed a curriculum that emphasizes the interdependence of everyone and everything. While the content of this curriculum is aligned to the traditional domains of educational knowledge, it is presented to children in unconventional ways.

In Chapter 5 we followed the developmental pathway from children's first sensory exploration of sound to their entry into the field of musical knowledge and the domain of musical culture. This chapter introduces other prepared paths to cultural knowledge in the Montessori curriculum.

Exploring the universe in the first years of school

When people stumble across keepsakes from childhood, they often find, in the laborious handwriting of those first years at school, an inscription such as the following in an old book or letter:

Elizabeth Jones
6 Smith St
Darlington
Sydney
Australia
The Southern Hemisphere
The Earth
The Solar System
The Milky Way
The Universe.

As adults we smile at this child of long ago locating herself so precisely in the universe. For Dr Montessori the intense interest children in the first years of school have for the whole universe, and their place in it, became the inspiration for the curriculum she designed for them, the curriculum she called 'Cosmic Education'.

Dr Montessori used the word 'cosmic' to draw attention to the orderly arrangement of the universe in which the children live. Through stories, lessons and games, children learn that everything in the universe, living and non-living, is interconnected and interdependent, and that everything and everyone, including themselves, has a contribution to make and a task to fulfil. The order and interdependency of all things in the universe becomes a metaphor for the classroom community the children build with their peers and the ethical questions they are encouraged to explore.

The Cosmic Education curriculum was designed in response to the challenges of Dr Montessori's time. Today Montessori educators argue that the ecological orientation of this curriculum is more important than ever. In the twenty-first century not only are we educating children for peace, but also for the sustainability of life on Earth.

A language for exploring the world

As we saw with the music curriculum, the Montessori path to educational knowledge has its origin in the infant's sensorial exploration, in Children's

House exercises of the auditory sense and in the language children learn to talk about pitch, sound quality and rhythm. Similarly, the prepared paths to domains of cultural knowledge such as geography, history, science and art, have their origins in the infant's sensory exploration and the exercises of the senses in the Children's House.

In the Children's House specialized vocabularies for talking about geography, history, science and art are introduced, so these areas of knowledge are treated as extensions of the language curriculum. Specialized terms appear in some sets of the vocabulary enrichment picture cards, for example, sets of animals, plants, different seasons, different parts of the world, aspects of the lives of people in all times and places, their clothes, buildings, transport and art. Children arrange the cards on a mat, sort them or match them to labels. The pictures inspire model-making, artwork and writing. Different topics feature in the classroom at different times, following children's evolving interests. Books in the library also cover these topics. This early language work evolves into the more differentiated Cosmic Education curriculum in the classroom for six- to nine-year-olds.

In the 'six to nine' classroom the topics of the Cosmic Education curriculum are presented in ways that highlight the links between each domain of knowledge. People live in different locations around the world (geography). Where they live, whether by the sea, on a river, a plain or mountain range, in hot or cool climates, determines the plants and animals in their environment (biology) and what happens to them over time (history). These factors, in turn, influence the food they eat, the clothes they wear, their means of shelter, transport and defence, and how they express themselves creatively and spiritually. Children can explore these interconnections in relation to themselves, or to other people around the world in our time and in the past. They can also use this approach to speculate about people's lives in the future.

Both in the Children's House, and as the Cosmic Education curriculum unfolds after the age of six, children are given language for talking about what they are learning in a very ordered and systematic way. They are given technical terms for different types of, for example, triangles, adjectives, vertebrates or valleys, as well as terms for parts of, for example, flowers, volcanoes or a starfish. Many of these words are scientific terms derived from ancient Greek and Latin. In the Children's House, in three-period lessons, children learn accurate, and often technical, names for the concrete objects they touch or trace. Three-period lessons continue for children over the age of six, but now they are also taught the etymology of words. In Montessori terms, etymology enables children to touch, with their imagination, the heart of a word. For example, 'corolla', the name for a part of a flower, has at its heart the meaning 'crown'.

The scope and sequence of the Montessori Cosmic Education curriculum is more comprehensive and more detailed than is usual in the early years of school. Montessori educators claim that presenting a view of the whole, then exploring the details and naming them with technical terms, captures the interest of young children. We often see this interest exploited by the toy industry. We are all familiar with how expert and engaged children can become in managing complex systems of collectable toys and cards. Montessori educators would argue that schools often neglect this 'sensitive period' instead of exploiting its full potential in the service of young children's education and development.

The Great Stories

When children make the transition from the Children's House into the classroom for six- to nine-year-olds, they are told a series of fables called the Great Stories. As seen in previous chapters the study of language and mathematics begins for six-year-olds with the great stories of the alphabet and numbers. In their first weeks in the new classroom, they are also told the story of the universe, a story that begins with the Big Bang and concludes with the formation of the Earth. As the curriculum unfolds, children hear stories about:

• the coming of life on Earth
• the coming of humans.

All these stories are scientifically and historically accurate, and orient children to discipline-based educational knowledge from an evolutionary and ecological point of view. The stories are told in a dramatic and theatrical way in order to transport the children, through their imaginations, beyond the confines of the classroom, to times before there were humans, or indeed any life at all on planet Earth, to the beginning of time itself, and to places anywhere on and beyond the Earth, to humans who came before us, known and unknown, whose discoveries and inventions have contributed to the way humans live today. The aim is to generate lots of questions and ideas for further research and exploration, to 'sow the seeds for the sciences' when children's capacity for imagination is at its height. Dr Montessori (1948/1973: 39) continues:

All is strictly interrelated on this planet. ... each detail holds the child's interest by reason of its strict relation to the others. We may compare it with a tapestry: each detail is a piece of embroidery; the whole constitutes a magnificent cloth.

The scope of the Montessori Cosmic Education curriculum cannot be captured in one short chapter. What follows serves as an introduction only to the ways children in Montessori schools work in the areas of science, geography and history, first in the Children's House and later in classrooms for children aged from six to nine.

Activity

In Montessori schools children of six are told the story of the universe. In other early childhood settings children of six often study the local neighbourhood.

If you were six, which approach would better capture and hold your attention and interest?

Describe the organization of a programme of study in the sciences and social sciences in an early childhood programme with which you are familiar. What are the most significant points of difference between this approach and the Montessori one?

Science

Science education plays a central role in Montessori classrooms, a legacy of Dr Montessori's scientific background.

Science in the Children's House

Science activities in the Children's House share many of the features of practical life exercises. All the objects needed for a science activity are colour-coded and placed together on a tray. They are all child-sized, but functional and kept clean and in perfect order. Children are given a presentation so they are able to do each activity independently, and clean up afterwards ready for the next person.

Science activities also share many of the features of the exercises of the senses. Using their senses, children have explored, largely unconsciously, in the home environment, phenomena such as gravity or light. These phenomena are isolated in the Montessori science activities so children begin to observe them consciously, separating them out as distinct objects of study from the otherwise undifferentiated background of experience.

Children are given the names of objects (e.g. magnet) and phenomena (e.g. sink, float) in spoken language lessons, often three-period lessons. If the topic captures children's interest, the teacher follows this interest, perhaps by creating manipulable materials based on a Montessori template that includes pictures, labels and little booklets with illustrations and short definitions. Books on the topic are also placed in the class library to encourage children's research. A person with expertise in the area might be invited to visit.

The repertoire of possible activities in physical science is extensive (gravity, light and shadow, air, magnetism, sound), but at any time a limited selection only is placed in the classroom, either to spark an interest or to follow one. Topics are changed regularly to maintain interest.

There is usually a nature table in the Children's House. On the table are displayed items of interest, contributed by the children or teacher (e.g. rocks, seed pods, shells, feathers, leaves), perhaps reflecting the season or a feature of the local environment. Ideally, the items should invite sensory exploration. The sense exercises give children a language to express their observations of, for example, shape, colour, texture, mass, temperature and size. If children show interest, the items on display might initiate classification activities and associated language lessons (e.g. types of rocks).

In the outdoors children observe living creatures in their habitat. The teacher models observation techniques that show respect and concern for the welfare of, and possible risks posed by, creatures that share our environment. Small field trips might be organized, for example, a nature walk to the local park or beach, especially if the children are likely to spot a particular animal, habitat, or plant at that time of day or year (e.g. rock pools, horses, flowering gum, spider webs, jellyfish, whales, sea eagles).

Science activities for children of this age are designed to instil a sense of wonder about different aspects of the world, as well as respect and empathy for living things.

Science in the Montessori classroom for six- to nine-year-olds

The curriculum for children aged from six to nine begins with the most breathtaking scientific story of them all, the story of the universe.

The story of the Big Bang and the formation of the Earth is accompanied by simple, but intriguing, experiments and coloured, illustrated charts. The story tells how, from the heat and light of the Big Bang, came everything we know. Spinning particles of gas cooled, and over vast stretches of time, coalesced into galaxies of stars. It is because all particles follow the laws of the universe that the planets spin around the Sun, and there are only three states of matter (solids, liquids and gases). As the Earth cooled, different substances turned into solids, liquids and gases at different temperatures. As gravity pulled them towards the centre of the Earth, each substance settled according to its weight, creating all the layers of the Earth: the heavy centre, the rocky crust, the oceans and the atmosphere.

After the story is told, the children try the experiments for themselves. The story is also the starting point for project work, for example, projects on the solar system, the layers of the Earth or any other aspect of the story the children find interesting. From this starting point, the curriculum fans out into the different domains of knowledge.

The prepared path to scientific knowledge is particularly rich in the Montessori 'six to nine' classroom. There are coloured charts, experiments, sets of pictures and movable materials, opening up endless possibilities for reading, manipulation, writing, art work, project work and field trips. Here are some examples:

- Children are told the story of the coming of life. They work with a chart on which the eras of the Earth's history are represented as a clock.
- The timeline of life is a very long chart illustrating, in pictures, the evolution of life from the Paleozoic Era (Ages of Invertebrates, Fishes and Amphibians), via the Mesozoic Era (Age of the Reptiles) to the Cenozoic Era (Age of Birds and Mammals). The chart has symbols for the ice ages, maps showing the movement of continents, red lines that trace the rise and fall of different types of plants and animals over time and labels for the eras and ages. The activities and project work associated with this chart are extensive.
- The study of the kingdoms of the Earth, the plant kingdom and the animal kingdom, are organized around illustrated classification charts, picture sets, labels and other manipulable material. Children learn the features of different types of plants and animals. The progression of this work is intertwined with work on the timeline of life.

The study of science in Montessori classrooms opens children's eyes to the wonders of planet Earth and the web of life it supports. The more children know about the Earth, Montessori educators believe, the more they will respect and care for it.

Case study 📁

In the 'six to nine' classroom the blank timeline of life is unrolled along the floor. Everyone steps round it, except William and Daniel at work sorting pictures of trilobites, crinoids, giant cephalopods, ferns, dinosaurs and early horses. Using the completed timeline mounted on the wall as control, they carefully place each picture in its right place along the evolutionary timescale. They pause when they find a picture of a giant dragonfly that lived during the Carboniferous period. A book in the library tells them the dragonfly was 70 cm long from wing tip to wing tip. They use the metre ruler to draw a 70 cm line along a large sheet of paper. Then they draw the outline of the giant dragonfly onto the line and cut out the shape. Now they see for themselves just how big this dragonfly really was!

Geography

The study of geography in the Children's House begins with small globes that children love to touch. Then they move onto the puzzle maps, a favourite work over extended periods of time.

Geography in the Children's House

Geography is a domain of knowledge with a particularly strong presence in the Children's House.

The globes

There are two Montessori globes, both with the oceans painted in glossy blue.

The land on the first globe is fine sandpaper. Once children perceive the difference between rough and smooth on the touch boards, at around age three, they are shown how to turn the globe very slowly as they touch the 'land' and the 'water', learning these words in a three-period lesson.

Children compare the first globe with the second globe, on which each continent is painted a different colour. With this globe children learn the words 'continent' and 'ocean'.

Land and water forms

The Montessori land and water forms are four pairs of small trays. In one of each pair of trays there is an earth-coloured mould of a land form and in the other its opposite water form. The pairs are:

- island and lake
- peninsula and gulf
- cape and bay
- isthmus and strait.

These are idealized representations, never models of land and water forms that actually exist. The activity itself is an extension of practical life. Children drop blue food colouring into a jug of water. They carefully pour water into each tray, so the images of the land and water forms come alive. They learn the names in three-period lessons. Follow up work includes:

- language enrichment:
  - pairing idealized pictures of land and water forms
  - working with two envelopes of aerial photographs (i.e. real-life examples), a green envelope for landforms, and a blue envelope for water forms
- using outline maps of the world, their own continent or other continents, children colour in land and water forms, one land or water form per map
- placing the labels for a land or water form on a blank map, checking against a control
- searching for land and water forms on maps and in atlases
- learning about archipelagos and chains of lakes.

Case study 📁

The land and water forms, and language to talk about them, have been presented to several children in the Children's House. In the following weeks, the language reappears in the children's own language:

- Jack is working with the puzzle map of the Oceania region. 'Hey, look!', he says, pointing to New Zealand. 'It's an island because it's surrounded by water.'
- Tom goes on a family holiday to Tasmania. He tells his teacher when he returns: 'It's an island because we went across the water.'
- Lowanna is on a ferry trip across the harbour with her father. She looks out and says, 'Look, that land is surrounded by water. It's an island.'

Puzzle maps

The puzzle maps are large wooden puzzles in which countries are the pieces. Each puzzle piece has a knob placed at the location of the capital city.

The first puzzle is a map of the world represented as two hemispheres. The puzzle pieces are the continents, in colours that match the painted globe. As children work with this map, they learn, in a three-period lesson, the names of the continents and the oceans. There are puzzle maps of the countries in the children's continent, the states or provinces in their own country, and the countries in each of the other continents.

There is also a set of colour-coded envelopes, one for each continent. In each envelope children find sets of pictures of people, plants and animals that live on that continent.

The puzzle map work continues for a long time. Children transfer their knowledge to work with real maps.

Case study 🗁

On our visit to the Children's House in Chapter 2 we see Bindi and Toby working together with a wooden map of Asia. Bindi has never done this map before. There are lots of very little pieces, and she is a bit confused, so Toby has come over to help. Toby is older and has completed this puzzle many times. He has even used the pieces as stencils to make his own map of Asia, a big work. He copied the names of his favourite countries onto the map, and some capital cities. He likes looking at books about Asia.

Both children are concentrating on picking up each little piece by the knob. Toby shows Bindi how to orient each piece, placing one corner down first so it slips into place.

Geography in the Montessori classroom for six- to nine-year-olds

The study of geography in the school years has its origin in the story of the formation of the Earth and the description of the layers of the Earth. Children make a special study of their own country, its place on the Earth, its land and water forms, its regions and cities and the work its people do. They then might do project work on another country or region of the Earth. Other geography topics include:

- the surface of the Earth (rocks, mountains, oceans, coasts, volcanoes)
- the Earth and the Sun (day and night, time zones, seasons, temperature zones)
- the work of air (atmosphere, wind, waves)

- the work of water (the water cycle, rivers, plains and valleys, waterfalls, glaciers)
- finding out about where everyday products come from (milk, bread, cotton, paper) and the work of the people who produce them for us.

Coloured charts, movable materials, model-making and project work accompany all these topics.

History

History in the Children's House
History in the Children's House follows on from the puzzle map work. More envelopes are prepared, for example, with images relating to the child's own continent, including pictures of people, things and events from earlier times. One continent or country and its history might become the focus of activities including art projects, writing, food preparation, displays, model-making or plays.

History in the Montessori classroom for six- to nine-year-olds
The origin of the study of history for children over six is intertwined with science in the telling of the first great stories. Parallel to the telling of these stories, the concept of time itself is explored from several perspectives.

- Children create timelines of their own lives.
- Movable material is used to explore the parts of the year (months, weeks, days).
- Long timelines are used to count back from the twenty-first century AD to centuries BCE.
- Children use a clock with movable pieces to learn about the parts of the day (hours, minutes, seconds) and to tell the time.
- Children unroll a long black line to discover a tiny sliver of white at the end. The white represents the very short amount of time humans have lived on the Earth.

A series of timelines, charts and movable materials is used to spark the children's interest in history and to generate research and project work.

The story of the coming of humans begins the study of human history, presented to the children as a continuation of the story of life on Earth. This story is accompanied by the timeline of humans, a long chart with illustrations showing stages of early human development (standing upright, using hands and the pincer grip, making tools and other artefacts, building shelter).

The study of history is organized around a picture chart of fundamental human needs, both material needs, such as food, shelter, clothing, transport, defence, and 'spiritual' needs such as art, religion and expressions of identity. Using this chart as a guide, children explore and compare the ways humans in different times and places have met their basic needs, from the time of early humans to the present. The history of the children's own country features in this work.

Organizing the study of history around the fundamental needs of humans has the following benefits:

• Children learn how much all humans have in common while at the same time they learn to understand and appreciate the different ways different groups of humans meet their needs.
• The chart foregrounds how dependent humans are on the resources of the three kingdoms of the Earth, the mineral kingdom, the plant kingdom and the animal kingdom. With this chart, the study of history and science again intersect. Children might research, for example, whether a particular group of humans used, or uses, plants, animals or minerals for food or clothing, transport or defence.

Visual arts

Visual arts in the Children's House
In the Children's House visual arts activities are set up in the same way as practical life exercises. All the materials and equipment needed for each activity are kept together on a tray. Children are shown how to do the activity and how to clean up.

Free work with media such as clay, paint or crayons is always available. In any week there is a limited selection of activities drawn from a larger repertoire, for example, sewing, weaving, printing or collage. These activities are often linked to what is happening in the classroom and the projects the children have initiated or have shown interest in.

Visual arts activities in the Children's House are an extension of the exercises of the senses. The inventory of sensory impressions isolated, organized and named during the exercises of the senses now become a source of inspiration and a resource for imaginative and creative expression. Observing children at work in the visual arts area reveals to teachers what children have gained from the exercises of the senses and which sense exercise to offer them next.

Many Montessori classrooms include sets of art appreciation cards. The pictures on these cards are artworks that are highly valued by people in the culture. Children use these pictures in matching and sorting activities. Quality prints, photographs and three-dimensional works are often placed in the environment as talking points. Art appreciation can be linked with the appreciation of different types of music, as well as the children's interests.

Visual arts in the Montessori classroom for six- to nine-year-olds

In Montessori classrooms for children older than six the visual arts are integrated into all areas of the curriculum. Research projects often involve model-making and illustration. They also inspire countless ideas for creative work. Groups will often work on visual arts projects together, for example, to create a mural, a mosaic or a backdrop for a play. Each new project motivates children to learn new skills and techniques with different media and art-making equipment. Children learn how to collect and organize their own equipment and how to clean up when they are finished. Art appreciation is extended, and linked with the study of history and geography.

Case study 🗀

The new six-year-olds in the 'six to nine' class have just heard the story of the formation of the Earth and the Solar System for the first time. They decide to build a model of the Solar System. They research the sun and planets, in the library and on the Internet. They prepare detailed descriptions in words and drawings. The teacher shows them how to make spheres from balloons covered in papier maché. Balloons are inflated to match the relative size of each planet, and the activity shifts to the art area. When the surfaces are dry, paint is mixed to match the colour of surfaces, and materials selected and fashioned to give each surface the right texture, whether of flame, rock, gas or ice. When the Solar System is finally hung from the ceiling, there are gasps of wonder all around.

Planning and programming

Echoing the Montessori mathematics curriculum, the lessons, exercises and activities of the Cosmic Education curriculum are grouped together around sets of materials related to a particular goal or topic. The first lesson of each topic presents children with an impression of the whole area of knowledge and the way it is organized, before they begin exploring the detail.

How does the teacher plan a programme of study when the curriculum is organized in this way?

• The first step is to select the goals and topics that will be introduced over a given school term or a year.
• The next step is to ensure the materials the children need to pursue that topic independently are prepared and placed in the environment.
• Finally children are presented with lessons that connect them to the material and set them up for independent work.

From that point the teacher observes children's work, selecting from the repertoire further lessons or activities on the basis of need or interest. Accurate record-keeping is an important component of this process.

Children's progress tends to be monitored within Montessori classrooms in terms of mastery, rather than the achievement of specific objectives, standards or outcomes. When children in Montessori schools are assessed against benchmarks set by external authorities, however, achievement levels align with, and often surpass, the required standards (Lillard and Else-Quest, 2006).

Summary ☐

The Montessori prepared paths to culture lead children from sensory exploration in infancy to educational knowledge in the school years. This chapter outlines the Montessori prepared paths that children follow to learn about the fields of science, geography, history and visual arts. As they follow these paths, children in Montessori schools are taught specialist and technical terms to talk with precision and in detail about the knowledge they are exploring. The precision and detail captures and holds their interest. The interdependency of all things, living and non-living, is emphasized as a means of educating children for peace and sustainability.

Things to think about

How are children in early childhood settings typically introduced to knowledge about science, geography, history and the visual arts?

Which of the topics, activities and techniques used in the Montessori approach to teaching educational knowledge in the early years could you adapt to your own teaching context and practice?

Montessori in context

Chapter objectives

- To locate the Montessori approach to early childhood education in a broader historical context.
- To link Dr Montessori's contribution to her predecessors and contemporaries in the field.
- To consider how Montessori ideas might contribute to the field of early childhood education into the future.

The first Montessori school opened one hundred years ago in the first decade of the twentieth century. In the first decade of the twenty-first century Montessori schools continue to flourish around the world. The method was originally devised for children of the slums, but in the last hundred years children of all backgrounds have attended Montessori schools. Uniquely among approaches to early childhood education in use today, the Montessori approach provides a bridge from the present to educational pioneers of centuries past, especially those who worked to make schools humane environments responsive to the developmental needs of children. Following the initial blaze of publicity surrounding the early breakthroughs in Montessori classrooms, the approach has never again been central to educational debates. Nevertheless, scattered through the literature of almost every decade of the last hundred years, there are references to Montessori education.

Bertrand Russell (1926: 35–7; 169–70) praised the active discipline in the Montessori classroom attended by his three-year-old son. A. S. Neill disagreed, arguing that the Montessori emphasis on order in early childhood cannot be good for young children. In his autobiography, the writer Gabriel García Márquez (2003: 94–5) describes how, as a child in Aracataca in tropical Colombia in the early 1930s, his difficulties with reading were overcome when he was taught his sounds the Montessori way, no doubt with sandpaper letters. Márquez praises the Montessori sense training as one of the best ways to make children 'sensitive to the beauties of the world' and curious about 'the secrets of life'.

Google 'Montessori' and you will sooner or later discover that the founders of Google.Inc were allowed to follow their own interests in Montessori schools before they made it so easy for everyone else to do the same online. Stay online and you will learn that, before he concentrated on books, the founder of Amazon.com concentrated in a Montessori preschool.

The Montessori approach emerged at a pivotal point in the history of early childhood education. As she designed her method, Dr Montessori surveyed the work of educational pioneers who preceded her in the eighteenth and nineteenth centuries. Her life's work was a response to the educational challenges of the twentieth century. As I hope this book has convinced you, her legacy continues to resonate in the twenty-first century.

This last chapter is written to 'sow seeds' of interest in the history of early childhood education. You might like to follow up any of these seeds in a research project of your own.

An influential story about an imaginary child

A book about the education of an imaginary child, Émile, written in eighteenth century France by Jean Jacques Rousseau (1762/1974), continues to exert influence on educators today. Rousseau describes an education in which Émile is kept away from society so his natural goodness and freedom are neither curtailed nor corrupted. As a young child, Émile explores the world with his senses, his exploration unspoiled by school learning, but kept in check by reality. It is only when he has grown through the natural stages of development, that Émile is ready to enter society.

At the end of the eighteenth century, a Swiss educator, Pestalozzi, designed an educational method based on Rousseau's ideas. His school had a homelike feel. There was no distinction between play and work, and children were free to choose from activities sequenced to match the stages of children's development.

Friedrich Froebel, the German founder of the kindergarten, visited Pestalozzi's school. There he saw children using manipulable objects designed to introduce them to abstract concepts. These objects became the inspiration for sets of manipulable solid geometric shapes that Froebel designed to enhance children's creative play. These sets of objects, which Froebel called *Gifts*, combined spheres, blocks, tiles, rings and sticks. Froebel is thought to be the first early childhood educator to give building blocks to children for free, creative play.

Why kindergarten and school are so different

While Froebel's influence is still felt in kindergartens and nursery schools today, it was another nineteenth century German educator, Herbart, whose ideas still shape the way schools are organized for older learners. Herbart also visited Pestalozzi's school, but his response was to design systematic teaching methods in which children begin studying a topic from a known starting point, and then progress steadily to the unknown. The teaching sequence begins with children being prepared for a topic. They are then presented with the topic and finally they apply what they have learned.

Activity

Some features of Montessori classrooms can be traced to these educational pioneers. Can you list these features?

Two nineteenth-century French doctors

As we have seen, Maria Montessori incorporated sensory education into her pedagogy, but not through the influence of Rousseau. On the whole, Maria Montessori thought Rousseau's ideas, and their implementation by Pestalozzi and Froebel, were impractical, especially for the disadvantaged children in her care. Education in this tradition gives children freedom to explore the environment through their senses, but they are given little external guidance on what to pay attention to and how to think about their discoveries. They have to rely largely on their own impulses and emotions. Herbart's approach, on the other hand, she thought would only work if children's interest were captured first. Rather than worrying about pouring things into children's minds, she believed educators should prepare environments that allow children to construct their intellect themselves. To find an approach that gave children freedom, but at the same time helped them adapt to society, Maria Montessori looked to the work of two little known nineteenth-century French doctors, Jean Itard and Edouard Séguin.

Jean Itard, a doctor like Maria Montessori, is famous as the teacher of Victor, the wild boy of Aveyron, a boy abandoned in a forest at about the age of four and found again when he was about twelve. When found, the child looked disgusting. He could not speak and twitched convulsively. He walked with a strange gait or ran on all fours. He bit and scratched like an animal, and could not focus his attention on anything. Most people thought the child could never be educated, but Dr Itard disagreed. Itard noticed that Victor's perception was limited to those things on which his survival depended. He could not, for example, distinguish hot from cold. This distinction held no meaning for him. He seemed not to hear a loud pistol shot, but did respond immediately when a walnut was cracked, a sound that, after all, meant food.

To teach Victor the difference between hot and cold, Itard gave him warm clothes, a warm bed and warm baths. Victor soon began to check the temperature of the bath water with his hand and to put on his own clothes to keep himself warm. Itard designed many playful activities to make distinctions such as soft and hard, rough and smooth, meaningful to Victor. Victor learned, for example, to check potatoes before he ate them to see if they were cooked.

Itard gradually drew Victor's attention to finer and finer contrasts in sounds, from the contrast between the sounds of a drum and a bell to the contrast between different sounds in the language.

Without external order Victor became distressed and disoriented, so Itard drew outlines to help the child order the objects in his room on hooks. Itard later used the same technique to teach Victor geometric shapes and the letters of the alphabet. Then he designed a series of activities based on grammar categories to teach Victor to read and write. While Victor made extraordinary progress, he never gained complete control of language and other social conventions in ways that were normal for children his age. Itard thought this was because he had missed critical developmental periods while he was isolated from society in the forest.

Edouard Séguin, a student of Itard, designed a sensory-based method for educating children who in those days were labelled 'idiots'. It was thought at the time that children with severe disabilities could not be educated, yet Séguin achieved remarkable results by combining movement with sensory training. In stark contrast to the asylums of the era, Séguin housed the children in pleasant surroundings, gave them nutritious food, warm clothing, and plenty of sleep, fresh air and exercise. They listened to music and took walks in the garden, and every effort was made to make them happy.

The key to teaching 'idiot' children, Séguin believed, was training their will. If they could control their movements and attention by themselves, they could take part in social life. He designed special materials and games to train movement and perception, all based on the principle of contrast, from the strongest contrasts to finer and finer distinctions. Then he turned his attention to training the intellect. When the children could perceive differences between the sounds of spoken language and the shapes of letters, Séguin devised a grammar-based method to teach them to read.

To teach educational knowledge, Séguin presented the children with meticulously designed concrete objects that embodied educational concepts. To give the children language to talk about the concepts, he designed a naming lesson in three parts. In this way the children experienced the concepts they were learning in multiple forms. Séguin (1866/1971: 182) summarized his approach in the following way:

> This juxtaposition or even identification of the three, four, or five forms of things, *i.e.*, their name written, printed, and pronounced, their images printed and carved, and their own selves in substance, such are the forcible instruments by which the first ideas may be forced through the senses into the mind.

It was Séguin's method that Montessori used so successfully in the 1890s to teach 'deficient' children at her institute in Rome. In 1907, when she adapted the same method to educate street children, she was amazed by what unfolded. The Montessori naming lesson is still known as the three-period lesson of Séguin.

Activity

Many of the features of Montessori classrooms can be traced to the work of Jean Itard and Edouard Séguin.
Can you list these features?

Maria Montessori's contemporaries

With her successful adaptation of Séguin's method in the first Children's House, Maria Montessori became a household name around the world, almost overnight. This instant celebrity generated a great deal of debate. Three well-known contemporaries of Dr Montessori, John Dewey, Jean Piaget and Lev Vygotsky, contributed to this debate. Here are some of the ways they evaluated her approach.

The American philosopher and educator, Professor John Dewey, met Maria Montessori in 1915 in New York. He introduced her to the record crowd who had come to listen to her talk about her method at Carnegie Hall. In that same year, John Dewey and his wife Evelyn Dewey published a book in which they discussed the Montessori method at length. The Deweys endorsed the following Montessori principles:

- When children are free to choose their own activity, the teacher can observe 'the needs and capabilities of each pupil' (Dewey and Dewey, 1915: 141).
- Positive discipline is developed through activity (Dewey and Dewey, 1915: 142–4).
- Material that is 'self-corrective' allows children to work independently (Dewey and Dewey, 1915: 153–4).
- The design of the Montessori 'apparatus' leads children to concentrate on the '*relations* between things' (Dewey and Dewey, 1915: 156–7; emphasis in the original).

While the Deweys agreed with the Montessori emphasis on liberty, they had 'a different conception of the best use to be made of it' (Dewey and Dewey, 1915: 157). They felt that Dr Montessori did not give children enough intellectual and creative freedom.

In the 1920s Jean Piaget conducted some of his earliest research in Geneva at a school that used a modified Montessori programme. Throughout the 1920s and 1930s Piaget kept in contact with the Montessori movement and knew Maria Montessori personally. Many years later Piaget (1970: 147–8) wrote that both Dewey and Montessori stood out from earlier educators because they incorporated into their approaches:

- 'work based on interest'
- 'activity providing training for thought'
- an understanding of development.

Maria Montessori in her work with 'abnormal pupils', according to Piaget (1970: 147–8), was 'confronted [...] with the most central questions of intellectual development', generalizing her discoveries 'with unparalleled mastery' to 'normal children' into a method 'whose repercussions throughout the entire world have been incalculable'.

The Montessori method has been evaluated from time to time against Piaget's developmental theories (Chattin-McNicholls, 1992; Elkind, 1974). Essentially, however, Montessori and Piaget were working on divergent projects. Piaget observed children's activity in order to build a theory of knowledge and its origins in childhood while Montessori observed children's activity in order to design pedagogy. The Montessori project is perhaps more fruitfully reviewed through the lens of the theories of Lev Vygotsky.

Maria Montessori was born more than two decades before the Russian psychologist Lev Vygotsky and she outlived him by another two decades, but they never met. Montessori never refers to Vygotsky in her writing. She may not have heard of him because his developmental psychology did not become well known in the West until after her death.

Vygotsky, however, was familiar with the ideas of both Séguin and Montessori. This is not surprising. In the early 1920s Vygotsky's interest in developmental psychology was aroused when he studied children with impaired development. Up to that time in Europe there were few educators who had done more than Séguin and Montessori to address the plight of these children.

The 'keystone' of Séguin's approach, Vygotsky (1935/1993: 218–20) writes, is 'free will'. If free will 'is impossible on the level of individual development, it becomes possible on the level of social development'. In addition, Vygotsky (1932/1993: 218) identifies Séguin as the source of the following insight:

> The developmental path for a severely retarded child lies through collaborative activity, the social help of another human being, who from the first is his mind, his will, his activities. This proposition also corresponds entirely with the normal path of development for a child.

Vygotsky studied children's development. He gave children tasks, then observed their activity, an approach similar to the one used by Montessori, but very different from the tightly controlled experiments more commonly used in psychology. When Vygotsky observed a phenomenon he called the zone of proximal development, he acknowledged that Montessori had recognized it first.

For each subject of instruction, there is a period when its influence is most fruitful because the child is most receptive to it. It has been called the *sensitive period* by Montessori and other educators (Vygotsky, 1934/1986: 189; emphasis in original).

A zone of proximal development, as described by Vygotsky (1978: 86) has two levels of development:

• the level at which a child can operate independently
• a 'level of potential development'.

The level of potential development is measured by what a child can do 'under adult guidance or in collaboration with more capable peers'. Children reveal this potential, when they, for example:

• imitate an adult to extend themselves 'well beyond the limits' of what they are capable of doing independently (Vygotsky, 1978: 88)
• engage in play oriented to what they can do in the future (Vygotsky, 1978: 102).

Vygotsky (1978: 117–18) used Montessori pedagogy as an example of the future-oriented play he had in mind:

Montessori has shown that kindergarten is the appropriate setting for teaching reading and writing, and this means that the best method is one in which children do not learn to read and write but in which both these skills are found in play situations. For this it is necessary that letters become elements in children's life in the same way, for instance, that speech is ... Reading and writing should become necessary for [the child] in her play.

This approach Vygotsky described as 'organised development rather than learning'. Other Vygotskian ideas that align with the Montessori approach, include the following:

• '[T]he environment is the source of development, not its setting' (Vygotsky, 1994: 347–9).
• By studying grammar, the school child becomes 'aware of what he is doing and learns to use his skills consciously' (Vygotsky, 1934/1986: 184).

Vygotsky was particularly interested in the role of activity and language in the evolution of children's thinking. His account of this evolution can be summarized in the following way.

When infants intentionally point at something, it usually means, 'I want you to look at this with me'. Gradually the action of pointing evolves into language. When children first use language, it is to single out something they are able to perceive, and to share that attention with others. Over time children begin to use language, not only to share with others what they perceive in the immediate here and now, but also to hold in their mind things they have perceived in other places and times. These 'memories' from the past, held in the mind in the shape of language, can be used to make decisions in the present, to plan for the future and to imagine new possibilities. Language has now become a tool for thinking.

Vygotsky contrasted the everyday knowledge children learn informally and randomly in daily life with the educational knowledge they learn in a systematic way at school. Educational knowledge, Vygotsky (1934/1986: 152) argues, does not prevent children's spontaneous activity, 'but rather charts new paths for it'.

Activity

Montessori pedagogy is built around sets of objects that 'materialize' educational knowledge in a concrete form children can manipulate with their hands. Children are shown how to use the objects and they are given very exact language to talk about the concepts the objects materialize. After the lesson children are free to work with the objects whenever they choose. Because the objects 'remember' the concepts in a form children can, literally, 'grasp', when children do choose to work with the objects, they are able to do so independently and for extended periods of time. As children grasp and manipulate the objects with their hands, they are learning how to grasp and manipulate the corresponding concepts in their minds.

How would you compare Montessori pedagogy with Vygotsky's account of the evolution of children's thinking?

The Montessori legacy

Maria Montessori (1946: 12) surrounded children with 'things to handle which in themselves convey steps in culture'. Then she left children free to follow their own interests. When children work with objects that interest them, independently and without interruption, she observed that they begin to concentrate and to exert control over their own movements and thoughts, no longer needing to be controlled by others. Furthermore, when children begin to concentrate, they become increasingly calm, focused and happy, a state Dr Montessori came to think of as the normal state of childhood. The more children were able to achieve this state, the more they were able to act, and interact, with confidence, respect and empathy.

The picture I have just painted represents, of course, the potential of the Montessori approach, and not always the reality. There is, obviously, enormous variety among the many thousands of Montessori schools around the world. Some schools are better administered and resourced than others, some teachers are better trained or have more experience than others. Montessori teachers, like teachers everywhere, have better days than others. Nevertheless, most Montessori teachers will tell you, based on their own experience, that when a Montessori classroom achieves its full potential, so do the children, and the teachers do too. Best of all, they say, the children love it.

Summary

By placing Maria Montessori's legacy in its historical context, it is possible to locate the origin of her approach to early childhood education in the work of the nineteenth century doctors, Jean Itard and Edouard Séguin. Her legacy is often compared with that of Jean Piaget, but, because her goal was to study the activity of young children in order to mediate more effectively in children's development, it can be argued that her legacy is perhaps more effectively evaluated using a Vygotskian framework.

Things to think about

Dr Montessori set out to solve one of the great riddles of early childhood education.
How do we give children the independence they crave while still giving them the tools to adapt to society?
Dr Montessori's legacy, based on a lifetime of observing young children's freely chosen activity, amounts to a detailed proposal for solving this riddle.
Do you agree?

Recommended reading

Britton, L. (1992) *Montessori Play and Learn: A Parent's Guide to Purposeful Play from Two to Six.* New York: Crown Publishers.

Cossentino, J. M. (2006) Big work: goodness, vocation, and engagement in the Montessori method. *Curriculum Inquiry* 36 (1): 63–92.

Duff, M. and Duffy, D. N. (2002) *Children of the Universe: Cosmic Education in the Montessori Elementary Classroom.* Hollidaysburg, PA: Parent Child Press.

Duffy, M. (2009) *Montessori Works: Montessori Math and the Developing Brain.* Altoona, PA: Parent Child Press.

Gettman, D. (1987) *Basic Montessori Learning Activities for Under-Fives.* New York: St Martin's Press.

Goertz, D. B. (2001) *Children Who are not yet Peaceful.* Berkeley, CA: Frog Ltd.

Isaacs, B. (2007) *Bringing the Montessori Approach to Your Early Years Practice.* New York: Routledge.

Kramer, R. (1978 [1976]) *Maria Montessori: A Biography.* Oxford: Basil Blackwell.

Lane, H. (1976) *The Wild Boy of Aveyron.* Cambridge, MA: Harvard University Press.

Lawrence, L. (1998) *Montessori Read and Write: A Parents' Guide to Literacy for Children.* London: Ebury Press.

Lillard, A. S. (2005) *Montessori: The Science Behind the Genius.* New York: Oxford University Press.

Lillard, A. S. and N. Else-Quest (2006) Evaluating Montessori education. *Science* 313, 29 September: 1893–4.

Lillard, P. P. (1996) *Montessori Today.* Chicago: Random House.

Lillard, P. P. and L. L. Jessen (2003) *Montessori from the Start: The Child at Home, from Birth to Age Three.* New York: Schocken.

Montessori, M. (1964 [1909, Italian/1912, English]) *The Montessori Method.* New York: Schocken Books.

Montessori, M. (1965 [1914]) *Dr Montessori's Own Handbook.* New York: Schocken Books.

Montessori, M. (1982 [1949]) *The Absorbent Mind,* 8th edn. Madras, India: Kalakshetra Publications.

O'Donnell, M. (2007) *Maria Montessori.* Continuum Library of Educational Thought, vol. 7. London and New York: Continuum.

Röhrs, H. (1994) Maria Montessori (1870–1952). *Prospects: The Quarterly Review of Comparative Education* (Paris, UNESCO: International Bureau of Education), vol. XXIV, no. 1/2 (89/90): 169–83. Available at: http://www.ibe.unesco.org/en/services/publications/thinkers-on-education.html

Seldin, T. and P. Epstein (2006) *The Montessori Way: An Education for Life*. Abingdon, MD: Consolidated Printing Company.

Standing, E. M. (1962 [1957]) *Maria Montessori: Her Life and Work*. New York: Mentor, New American Library of World Literature.

Waller, T. and R. Swann (2009) Children's learning, in T. Waller (ed.) *An Introduction to Early Childhood*, 2nd edn. London: Sage, pp. 31–46.

Recommended videos

Haines, A. (2004) *Maria Montessori: Her Life and Legacy*. DVD. San Luis Obispo, CA: Davidson Films.

Lillard, A. L. (2006) *Montessori: The Science Behind the Genius*. DVD. Paladin Pictures.

Recommended websites

Montessori organizations

Association Montessori Internationale (AMI), http://www.montessori-ami.org/

From this website you can follow links to Montessori organizations around the world. You will also find a wealth of information about Montessori education and its history, as well as teacher training.

Montessori World Educational Institute (MWEI), http://www.montessoriworld.org/

This website includes detailed information about Montessori materials and exercises, with illustrations. It also includes video recordings of a teacher trainer who was trained by Maria Montessori herself, demonstrating the materials and their use for trainee teachers.

For information about the work of Educateurs sans Frontiers, see http://ww.montessori-ami.org/esf/esf.htm

Montessori publications

Montessori Books, http://www.montessoribooks.com.au/

Parent Child Press, http://www.parentchildpress.com

Itard and Séguin

Jean Itard (1802) *An historical account of the discovery and education of a savage man*. London: Richard Phillips. http://www.feralchildren.com/en/pager.php?df=phillips1802

Séguin, E. (1866) *Idiocy and its Treatment by the Physiological Method*. New York: William Wood and Company. Available online at: http://books.google.com.au/books?id=9uFb0xDxHV4C&printsec=titlepage&output=html

Montessori materials

Nienhuis Montessori (The Netherlands), http://www.nienhuis.com.

Gonzagarredi (Italy), http://www.gonzagarredi.it/english/settori/montessori.html

KayBee Montessori (India), http://www.montessoricollection.com/

General

Wikipedia entries on Larry Page and Sergey Brin, the founders of Google, attending Montessori pre-schools:

http://en.wikipedia.org/wiki/Larry_Page#Early_life_and_education

http://en.wikipedia.org/wiki/Sergey_Brin#Early_life_and_education

A description of the single-mindedness of Jeff Bezos, the founder of Amazon.com, at his
   Montessori pre-school:
http://www.businessweek.com/magazine/content/04_51/b3913022_mz072.htm
For information about Friedrich Froebel and the Froebel *Gifts*:
http://www.froebelweb.org/
http://geocities.com/froebelweb/gifts/index.html

Bibliography

Chattin-McNicholls, J. (1992) *The Montessori Controversy.* Albany, NY: Delmar.

Cossentino, J. M. (2006) Big work: goodness, vocation, and engagement in the Montessori method. *Curriculum Inquiry* 36 (1): 63–92.

Dewey, J. and E. Dewey (1915) *Schools of Tomorrow.* London: Dent and Sons.

de Winter, M. (2003) On infantilization and participation: pedagogical lessons from the century of the child, in W. Koops and M. Zuckerman (eds) *Beyond the Century of the Child: Cultural History and Developmental Psychology.* Philadelphia: University of Pennsylvania Press, pp. 159–82.

Elkind, D. (1974) Montessori and Piaget, in *Children and Adolescents: Interpretive Essays on Jean Piaget* (2nd edn). New York: Oxford University Press, pp. 128–38.

Feez, S. (2007) Montessori's Meditation of Meaning: a social semiotic perspective (Unpublished PhD thesis. University of Sydney) Available at: http://hdlhandle. net/2123/1859

Feez, S. (2008) Multimodal representation of educational meanings in Montessori pedagogy, in L. Unsworth (ed.) *Multimodal Semiotics: Functional Analysis in Contexts of Education.* London and New York: Continuum, pp. 201–15.

Fleer, M. and L. Surman (2006) A sociocultural approach to observing and assessing, in M. Fleer, S. Edwards, M. Hammer, A. Kennedy, A. Ridgeway, J. Robbins and L. Surman, *Early Childhood Communities: Sociocultural Research in Practice.* Frenchs Forest, NSW: Pearson Education Australia, pp. 141–60.

García Márquez, G. (2003) *Living to Tell the Tale* (Translated by E. Grossman). London: Jonathan Cape.

Grazzini, C. (1996) The four planes of development. *The NAMTA Journal* 21 (2): 208–41.

Haines, A. (2004) *Maria Montessori: Her Life and Legacy.* DVD. San Luis Obispo, CA: Davidson Films.

Kramer, R. (1978 [1976]) *Maria Montessori: A Biography.* Oxford: Basil Blackwell.

Kripalani, L. (1987) Observation, in *Communications: Journal of the Association Montessori Internationale* (1987/1) Amsterdam: AMI: 2–11.

Lane, H. (1976) *The Wild Boy of Aveyron.* Cambridge, MA: Harvard University Press.

Lillard, A. S. (2005) *Montessori: The Science Behind the Genius.* New York: Oxford University Press.

Lillard, A. S. and N. Else-Quest (2006) Evaluating Montessori education. *Science* 313, 29 September: 1893–4.

MacNaughton, G. and G. Williams (2004) *Techniques for Teaching Young Children: Choices in Theory and Practice*, 2nd edn. Frenchs Forest, NSW: Pearson Education Australia.

Miller, J. K. (1981) The Montessori music curriculum for children up to six years of age. Unpublished PhD thesis, Case Western Reserve University.

Montessori, M. (1946) *Education for a New World*. Madras, India: Kalakshetra Publications.

Montessori, M. (1964 [1909, Italian/1912, English]) *The Montessori Method*. New York: Schocken Books.

Montessori, M. (1965a [1914]) *Dr Montessori's Own Handbook*. New York: Schocken Books, pp. 9–24.

Montessori, M. (1965b [1916, Italian/1918, English]) *The Advanced Montessori Method: Scientific Pedagogy as Applied to the Education of Children from Seven to Eleven Years, Volume 1. Spontaneous activity in education*. Madras, India: Kalakshetra Publications.

Montessori, M. (1967 [1948, Italian]) *The Discovery of the Child*. New York: Ballantine Books. (A revision of *The Montessori Method* first published in 1909.)

Montessori, M. (1971 [1943]) *Peace and Education*. Madras, India: The Theosophical Publishing House, Adyar.

Montessori, M. (1971 [1934 in Spanish]) *Psicoaritmetica: l'aritmetica sviluppata secondo le indicazioni della psicologia infantile durante venticinque anni di esperienze*. Translated into Italian by C. Grazzini. Milan: Garzanti, vii–xvi.

Montessori, M. (1973 [1948 French]) *From Childhood to Adolescence*. New York: Schocken Books.

Montessori, M. (1982 [1949]) *The Absorbent Mind*, 8th edn. Madras, India: Kalakshetra Publications.

Montessori, M. (1983 [1936]) *The Secret of Childhood*. London: Sangam Books.

Montessori, M. (1994 [1939]) *Creative Development in the Child* (Volume I). Madras, India: Kalakshetra Publications.

Montessori, M. (1997 [1915]) *The California Lectures of Maria Montessori, 1915: Collected Speeches and Writings*. Edited by R. G. Buckenmeyer. The Clio Montessori Series Volume 15. Oxford: Clio Press.

Montessori, Mario. (1965) Foreword, in M. Montessori (1965 [1918]), *The Advanced Montessori Method*. Madras, India: Kalakshetra Publications, pp. vii–xiii.

Montessori, Mario M. (1976) *Education for Human Development: Understanding Montessori*. New York: Schocken Books.

Murray, J. (2009) Studying the worlds of young children: knowing and understanding, in T. Waller (ed.) *An Introduction to Early Childhood*, 2nd edn. London: Sage, pp. 138–51.

Organization of Economic Cooperation and Development Centre for Educational Research and Innovation (OECD CERI) (2007) *Understanding the Brain: The Birth of a Learning Science*. Paris: OECD.

Piaget, J. (1970) *Science of Education and the Psychology of the Child*. Harmondsworth, Middlesex: Penguin Books.

Rambusch, N. (1965) Introduction, in M. Montessori (1965 [1914]) *Dr Montessori's Own Handbook*. New York: Schocken, pp. 9–24.

Rousseau, J. J. (1974 [1762]) *Émile or On Education* (Translated by B. Foxley). London: Dent.

Russell, B. (1926) *Education and the Good Life*. New York: Boni & Liveright.

Séguin, E. (1971 [1866]) *Idiocy and its Treatment by the Physiological Method*. New York: Augustus M. Kelley.

Standing, E. M. (1962 [1957]) *Maria Montessori: Her Life and Work*. New York: Mentor, New American Library of World Literature.

Vygotsky, L. S. (1978) *Mind in Society: The Development of Higher Psychological Processes*. Cambridge, MA: Harvard University Press.

Vygotsky, L. S. (1986 [1934]) *Thought and Language*. Cambridge, MA: The MIT Press.

Vygotsky, L. S. (1993 [1932]) Introduction to E. K. Gracheva's book: *The Education and Instruction of Severely Retarded Children*. In R. W. Rieber and A. S. Carton (eds), *The Collected Works of L. S. Vygotsky. Volume 2. The Fundamentals of Defectology (Abnormal psychology and learning disabilities)* (Translated by J. E. Knox and C. B. Stevens). New York and London: Plenum Press, pp. 212–19.

Vygotsky, L. S. (1993 [1935]) The problem of mental retardation, in R. W. Rieber and A. S. Carton (eds), *The Collected Works of L. S. Vygotsky. Volume 2. The Fundamentals of Defectology (Abnormal psychology and learning disabilities)* (Translated by J. E. Knox and C. B. Stevens). New York and London: Plenum Press, pp. 220–40.

Vygotsky, L. S. (1994) The problem of the environment, in R. van der Veer and J. Valsiner (eds), *The Vygotsky Reader*. Oxford, UK and Cambridge, USA: Blackwell, pp. 338–54.

Waller, T. and R. Swann (2009) Children's learning, in T. Waller (ed.), *An Introduction to Early Childhood*, 2nd edn. London: Sage, pp. 31–46.

Index